PRAISE FOR *REG*

"What I love about *Regroup* is that it doesn't just inspire, it equips. Barbara gives leaders tools to stay grounded in who they are, so they can ignite purpose in others. Her blend of science, story, and heart makes this a guide for anyone leading through both vision and challenge. This isn't about pushing harder; it's about leading from a deeper place of strength."

—Dr. Kary Oberbrunner
CEO of Igniting Souls and Instant IP
Wall Street Journal and *USA Today* Bestselling Author

"*Regroup* is a powerful reminder that being a force for good starts at home. Barbara Gustavson shows how reclaiming your energy and clarity can ripple outward, increasing your positive impact. You'll love this grounding, deeply inspiring book."

—Sam Horn
Founder of the Force for Good Project
Author of *Talking on Eggshells*

"Barbara has an exceptional ability to make complex ideas clear and practical. *Regroup* is a trusted companion for leaders and coaches carrying invisible weight while staying true to their mission. Blending neuroscience, story, and soul, she offers a powerful framework for sustainable leadership."

—Ellin Sidell
Author, Leadership Coach, and
Creator of The Sidell Method

"*Regroup* captures you from the very first line. It is that compassionate, loving voice, desperately needed by all caregivers, whether it's traditional ones, such as a nurse, or non-traditional ones, such as those taking care of an aging parent. It speaks truth to the invisible weight that all caregivers carry, especially in a world where we are praised for pushing harder. And during these times of great instability across the planet, the stressors that caregivers shoulder are even greater. What is so beautiful about *Regroup* is the humanness in the storytelling. It gives you permission to reconnect to yourself and give yourself that breath. You will feel seen, heard, and honored. This book gives you love, inspiration, and tools to be able to regroup and start to release that invisible weight."

—**Cindy Khoury Ashton**
Award-Winning TV Host, Singer/Actor, Entertainer
High Performance Speaking Strategist

"In a culture that often equates worth with constant motion and achievement, Barbara offers restorative alternatives that are rooted in practical steps and encouragement to pause, reflect, and realign. She shares personal challenges that illuminate the complexity of our human experience, offering wise, actionable guidance to rest, reset, and rediscover the joy of living. Her voice is grounding and uplifting, reminding us that healing is not a detour but an essential part of our journey."

—**Lisa Wetzel**
President & CEO of VIKINT

"Barbara's book is a timely and much-needed resource for anyone carrying the weight of too many responsibilities. As an occupational therapist, I see firsthand how stress and overwhelm can slowly erode a person's energy, focus, and, ultimately, their health. What I love about *Regroup* is that it offers clear, brain-based strategies that are both practical and easy to apply in everyday life. Barbara beautifully gives words to what so many people feel but struggle to articulate."

—**Tammy R. McKee**, MS, OTR/L, CHT
Owner of Hands Above Therapy Services

REGROUP

How to Reset Your Mind So
You Experience Untapped Energy,
Enjoy Productive Peace,
and Feel Like Yourself Again

REGROUP

HOW TO RESET YOUR MIND SO
YOU EXPERIENCE UNTAPPED ENERGY,
ENJOY PRODUCTIVE PEACE,
AND FEEL LIKE YOURSELF AGAIN

Barbara Gustavson

ethos
collective

Printed in the United States of America

Published by Igniting Souls
PO Box 43, Powell, OH 43065
IgnitingSouls.com

LCCN: 2025919552
Paperback ISBN: 978-1-63680-565-8
Hardback ISBN: 978-1-63680-566-5
eBook ISBN: 978-1-63680-567-2

Available in paperback, hardcover, e-book, and audiobook.

All Scripture quotations, unless otherwise indicated, are taken from the Holy Bible, New International Version®, NIV®. Copyright © 1973, 1978, 1984, 2011 by Biblica, Inc.™ Used by permission of Zondervan. All rights reserved worldwide. www.zondervan.com The "NIV" and "New International Version" are trademarks registered in the United States Patent and Trademark Office by Biblica, Inc.™

Any Internet addresses (websites, blogs, etc.) and telephone numbers printed in this book are offered as a resource. They are not intended in any way to be or imply an endorsement by Igniting Souls, nor does Igniting Souls vouch for the content of these sites and numbers for the life of this book.

Some names and identifying details may have been changed to protect the privacy of individuals.

The content of this book reflects the author's personal experiences, opinions, and interpretations. The inclusion of any individual, living or deceased, or any organization or entity, is not intended to malign, defame, or harm the reputation of such persons or entities. All statements regarding individuals are solely the author's perspective and do not represent verified facts unless expressly cited to a verifiable source.

The publisher has not independently investigated or confirmed the accuracy of any such references and disclaims all responsibility for them. Nothing in this book should be construed as factual assertions about the character, conduct, or reputation of any individual or entity mentioned. Any resemblance to persons living or dead is purely coincidental unless explicitly stated.

The publisher expressly disclaims liability for any alleged loss, damage, or injury arising from any perceived defamatory content or reliance upon statements within this work. Responsibility for the views, depictions, and representations rests solely with the author.

The superscript symbol IP listed throughout this book is known as the unique certification mark created and owned by Instant IP[IP]. Its use signifies that the corresponding expression (words, phrases, chart, graph, etc.) has been protected by Instant IP[IP] via smart contract. Instant IP[IP] is designed with the patented smart contract solution (US Patent: 11,928,748), which creates an immutable time-stamped first layer and fast layer identifying the moment in time an idea is filed on the blockchain. This solution can be used in defending intellectual property protection. Infringing upon the respective intellectual property, i.e., IP, is subject to and punishable in a court of law.

Disclaimer: This book is provided for educational and informational purposes only and does not constitute providing or substitute for medical advice or professional or mental health services. The information provided should not be used for diagnosing or treating a health problem, and those seeking personal medical advice should consult with a licensed physician. Always seek the advice of your doctor or other qualified health provider regarding a medical condition.

Dedication

For every supporter, caregiver, and leader
who quietly carries more
than most will ever know—this book is for you.
May you give yourself the same support
you give to others so freely.

You can access exclusive REGROUP bonuses by submitting the order number from your book purchase receipt at discovernextstep.com/regroup-book.com.

Table of Contents

PART 3: REBUILD

APPENDIX

Foreword

I am honored to write the foreword for Barbara Gustavson's remarkable new book, *Regroup*. Barbara has taken a message that is both timeless and urgently needed—how to recover from the creeping depletion that hides behind high performance—and shaped it into a clear, compassionate, brain-based roadmap that leaders, caregivers, and health professionals can use today.

Too many of us have learned to run on fumes. We praise hustle and stamina while neglecting the very organ that makes everything possible: the brain. Barbara's work is a welcome fix.

Regroup is not another pep talk; it is a practical, science-informed guide that marries the neuroscience I've spent my career studying with the real-world strategies people need to restore energy, clarity, and joy.

What I love most about *Regroup* is its foundation in brain-first thinking. The book doesn't ask you to change overnight or to add a dozen new habits at once. Instead, Barbara offers a simple, memorable framework—R.E.G.R.O.U.P.— that walks you from inner awareness to lasting repair.

This framework is grounded in how the brain actually works. When we restore sleep, reduce inflammation, calm the nervous system, and repair relationships, brain circuits heal. When we practice new, constructive thoughts instead of automatic negative thoughts (ANTs), we literally rewire our brains for greater resilience. That's not just hopeful language; it's neuroscience that translates into everyday choices.

Barbara's voice is both wise and warm. She writes with the authority of a facilitator who has worked hand in hand with leaders at the edge of burnout—and with the humility of someone who understands how hard change can be. Her exercises and case examples are highly usable: short, tangible practices you can fold into a busy week. From breathwork and margin-setting to cognitive reframes and prioritizing restorative sleep, Barbara gives you tools that actually work.

If you are a leader who feels exhausted but compelled to keep going, Regroup will help you stop running on empty and start leading from a place of strength. If you are a clinician or coach, you will find a clinical lens that respects both science and the human heart. And if you are simply someone who wants to feel like yourself again, this book meets you exactly where you are with encouragement, clarity, and doable steps forward.

Barbara's work continues the mission we share at Amen Clinics and Amen University: to bring brain health into everyday life so that people can do more of what matters: loving well, thinking clearly, and living with purpose. Regroup is a vital contribution to that mission.

Read it, practice it, and pass it along. You don't have to be broken to benefit from this book—you only need to be ready to take the small, powerful steps that restore your life. Barbara will show you how.

—Dr. Daniel Amen
Founder of Amen Clinics, BrainMD, Amen University, and
Change Your Brain Foundation

PART 1

RECOGNIZE

Chapter One

The Tug
You Can't Ignore

*You can't truly show up for others
if you're disappearing from yourself.*

—Dr. Caroline Leaf

I'LL NEVER FORGET sitting across the table from my dad at Cracker Barrel when he slid a folded paper across the table at the restaurant and grinned. "Look! We're famous." It was a tabloid magazine, and the headline read "ANCESTRY. BOMB." Beneath it was an old black-and-white photo of my great-grandfather and my grandfather with a collection of familiar relatives.

We were supposed to be enjoying Thanksgiving dinner. Instead, that headline pulled me into a family story of murder, a cover-up, suicide, mental illness, and a common link tying several of them to Huntington's disease, which impacts the brain.

Immediately, I wondered if my dad had it too. Hundreds of emotions flooded me: shock, anger, shame, grief. Being thankful wasn't one of them.

That experience pulled back the curtain on something bigger, and I felt the kind of gut-punch you can't ignore. I suddenly recognized how life pressures, old stories, and invisible weight quietly shaped the way I lived and thought.

That moment shifted something in me. It wasn't just the shock of what I learned; it was the weight I'd been carrying without even realizing it. I started questioning everything, even my calling. I couldn't figure out why the work I cared about started to feel harder. Why did I feel tired and anxious even when I was doing what I loved?

Have you ever carried a weight you couldn't name? The quiet doubt. The frustration. The sense that no matter what you do, something still feels off.

You look fine on the outside. You're the one others lean on. You keep showing up at work and in your relationships, but underneath it all, there's a different story unfolding—a story of fatigue, weight, or pain that most don't see. You're strong, yes. But having strength doesn't mean you're not suffering. The question isn't whether someone else will step up for you. The question is: Will you choose to step up and be a voice for yourself?"

That's where my story begins.

Your Heart Signals the Truth

This isn't a book about pushing harder. It's not another "go big or go home" message wrapped in pretty language. That approach has been done. We've read the books, tried the tips, and followed the frameworks. And yet, so many continue to feel the symptoms of burnout. We wonder *why*, when we're doing all the right things, something still feels off.

Deep inside, you know the truth. *This isn't working.*

I've felt it too. That inner tug-of-war between purpose and pressure isn't just stress; it's a signal. It's your heart's way of calling you back to what matters.

Eight years before that Cracker Barrel moment, my mom suffered a stroke. I spent my time supporting and advocating for her. Miraculously, she survived. But shortly after she was released from rehab, it happened again. This time, she didn't recover.

Suddenly, I became the full-time decision-maker for my dad. I didn't realize just how much Mom had been carrying behind the scenes. She had quietly taken on the role of caregiver, managing his medications, appointments, and daily needs, all without letting on how serious things had been.

After she passed, my dad had no idea what medications he was on or who his doctor was. My mom had handled it all. And now, everything fell to me.

That moment was the beginning of a new kind of life— one built around emergencies, uncertainty, and the weight of responsibility I wasn't prepared for. My sister couldn't help due to her own brain health struggles, and while my husband was incredibly supportive, it was still a lot to carry.

And in the middle of it all, I worked. I loved my job. It gave me purpose. It had taken me decades to find a career that felt meaningful. But the tug-of-war between caregiving, parenting, and building a business wore me down. Over time, my health took a hit. I went through at least two clear bouts of burnout and questioned whether I could keep going. At times, the cost seemed too high. I felt guilty for wanting to grow my business while my dad was struggling, yet I also felt called to make an impact. That tension haunted me every day.

Eventually, I began to ask a different question: *What if I didn't have to choose between the people I love and the work I'm called to do? What if there's a better way?*

That question led me to step back, reevaluate how I was operating—emotionally and physically—and take a hard look at what needed to change. In some areas of my life, I honestly did not feel the "burnout." But in other areas, they whispered softly, "This isn't working." I call it, *invisible weight.*

> That quiet tug in your heart isn't failure. It's aliveness

Do you ever feel that quiet tug in your heart—the one that whispers something needs to change? That's not failure. That's aliveness. It's your brain, body, and spirit trying to get your attention and inviting you toward something better.

Invisible, but Heavy

Maybe you're carrying invisible weight too. Chronic stress no one else can see. Caregiving responsibilities don't come with a clock-out time. Or perhaps you grapple with the load of perfectionism, quietly tying your worth to how well you perform, manage, or hold it all together. Maybe you're worried you've lost your edge. This book is for you.

You're not imagining it; the struggle is real. And it's wearing you down.

I know. We've been conditioned to believe doubling down will fix it. Just be more disciplined. Push harder. But what if that mindset actually keeps us stuck?

Let's look at the facts:

- A 2021 American Psychological Association study found that nearly three in five employees reported negative impacts of work-related stress, including decreased motivation and energy.[1]

- Research shows that 40 percent to 70 percent of family caregivers experience significant symptoms of depression, and up to half may meet criteria for major clinical depression.[2]
- Burnout is common even among high performers—people who look "fine" on the outside but are quietly unraveling on the inside.[3]

But what if there's a different way? What if it's not about time management, squeezing more into your day, or hacking your calendar?

What if the solution isn't in pushing forward, but in pulling back—not in defeat, but in clarity?

The answer is to *regroup.*

When I say regroup, you might picture a military tactic—dropping back, reorganizing, and moving forward with renewed strength. Regrouping our lives isn't all that different. To regroup means pausing and realigning with what matters most, especially after disruption or depletion.

> I've never met a strong person with an easy past.

Regrouping doesn't mean abandoning responsibilities or shutting down. It's taking an intentional step back to gather your strength and focus so you can reset and step back in with more direction and clarity. Someone once said, "I've never met a strong person with an easy past." Regrouping helps us reclaim clarity in the midst of chaos and remain strong when life feels heavy.

This space between exhaustion and renewal—between holding it all together and learning how to live from a place of strength again—gives us an opportunity to listen. Not just to our goals, but to our gut. Not only to what's urgent, but to what's meaningful. That tug you feel means something inside you is asking for a better way.

My first book, *Permission to Be Bold,* explored the small steps that free you to be yourself. This book invites you to give yourself permission to regroup—to take care of yourself, to pause, reset, and gather your strength so you can move forward with more clarity and peace. Think of it as a fresh start, not because everything changes, but because you change. *How?* You start thinking differently and build new habits—and new habits change behavior.

Reflection

At the end of each chapter, I'll invite you to pause and reflect. Sometimes we move so fast and push so hard, we don't recognize the tug-of-war going on inside. This is your opportunity to be still, breathe, and build a new habit.

- What parts of your life feel like they're pulling you in different directions?
- What part of you has been silently carrying weight no one else sees?
- Where do you find yourself trying to hold "it" all together?
- Do you make time to care for yourself, or does it only happen when everything else is done?
- What would life look like to be able to speak up for yourself?

Be honest with yourself. Your answers reveal how important this is.

Chapter Two

Stress, Overwhelm, and the Quiet Build of Burnout

Listen to the whisper.
Don't wait for the 2x4.

—A wise mentor

EVERYONE FACES AN internal tug-of-war at some point, and it comes with a variety of symptoms. Your vision narrows. Life feels gray and flat. What once brought joy feels muted. Going through the motions, you get things done, but it's as if life has lost its color. These are just a few of the many symptoms of prolonged stress, overwhelm, and burnout. Unfortunately, most leaders have become experts at pushing through, hiding the pain, and ignoring the whisper.

Burnout isn't a character flaw, and stress is not the villain; they're symptoms of your body and brain experiencing pressure. Many don't recognize the quiet build and subtle signals. Our nervous systems, emotional loads, and thought patterns all play a role. They shape how you're showing up every day.

Burnout is your brain saying, *This is too much, too fast, for too long.* But believe it or not, not all stress is bad or leads to burnout.

The Different Faces of Stress

In *The Upside of Stress,* psychologist Kelly McGonigal explains that how we view stress shapes how it affects us. Stress can actually prepare us for challenge, growth, and meaning. Yet we're often told to eliminate it altogether. That goal sets us up for frustration, because it's simply not possible. If you're living and breathing, stress will show up. What matters is learning to work with the right kind of stress and at the right level.[4]

This means the goal isn't to get rid of stress but to change how we think about it. When we stop fighting its existence, we can start recognizing its different forms. Not all stress is destructive. Some of it—including the kind that makes your heart race—can be life-giving. Researchers often describe two faces of stress:

- **Eustress** sharpens focus, fuels motivation, and helps you rise to the occasion. Think of the nerves you feel before giving a presentation or the drive that comes with caring deeply about something. This stress says you're alive, engaged, and growing.
- **Distress** drains you. It's the chronic, prolonged, heavy load without time for recovery. This stress overwhelms the nervous system, shrinks creativity, and erodes your sense of self. Left unchecked, it can pave the road to burnout.[5]

For years, I tried to get rid of my stress, not realizing that the harder I fought it, the more stressed I became. Someone once said, "You can't fix what you can't face." But what if we need to face the fact that we might be creating more stress by believing it shouldn't be there in the first place?

I've learned that one key isn't to avoid stress but to pay attention to how my body is responding while experiencing stress. When stress becomes constant, cortisol can flood your system and stay elevated. The prefrontal cortex—the part of your brain responsible for clarity, planning, and regulation—starts to dim. Your brain flips into survival mode. Creativity shrinks. Patience thins. Even simple tasks and decisions feel monumental.

> Stress isn't always a threat. Often, it's a message.

This does not mean you're broken. Your brain and body are designed to communicate under pressure. Stress isn't always a threat. Often, it's a message. It might be telling you that something matters or a sign that your body is equipping you to meet a challenge.

Understanding stress—what kind it is and what it's telling you–can help you determine whether you're on the path towards growth, or if something needs to change so you can avoid burnout.

The Body Keeps Score

Frequent overwhelm is often a sign of unchecked stress. And it doesn't just live in the mind. It also shows up in the body. If you feel constantly tired, even after a full night's sleep, or find yourself with headaches or stomach aches more often, it may be due to chronic stress. Pay attention if you get sick easily or your body feels like it's trudging through mud.

You might see a shift in emotions too. Some describe it as being "on edge." Others feel like they're moving through life on autopilot. If you're overreacting to small things, crying more than usual, or snapping at people you love, it could be your body waving the flag of surrender.

The symptoms might be pointing to compassion fatigue. Without awareness, overwhelm and compassion fatigue can sneak up on us. Helpers, caregivers, and leaders experience this real form of stress in growing numbers. According to the *Journal of Advanced Nursing*, individuals with high empathy are more susceptible to burnout due to their emotional investment. When we consistently absorb others' struggles without replenishing our own reserves, the load becomes too heavy, and empathy slowly shifts into exhaustion.[6] The very thing that makes you good at what you do—caring—makes you vulnerable to collapse if you ignore the signs.

As psychiatrist Bessel van der Kolk explains in *The Body Keeps the Score*, our bodies hold on to stress and struggle even when our minds try to push through. The body "keeps the score" by carrying the stress in the form of tension, illness, or exhaustion. Your physical body often speaks before you do.[7] And if you don't listen, burnout will speak louder.

The Subtle Drift

The World Health Organization calls burnout "a syndrome resulting from chronic workplace stress that has not been successfully managed." That definition fits, but it misses the way personal stress and overwhelm contribute to the problem. Burnout drains your sense of self.

Burnout and the path there offer at least five signs:

- You're exhausted, but can't seem to rest.
- Things that used to bring joy now feel flat.
- Your patience is paper-thin.
- You feel more emotional than usual or more shut down.
- You wonder, "What's wrong with me?"

These physical signs are whispers. Paying attention to them is how you begin to regroup and reduce the chances of severe burnout.

When you feel exhausted, your brain is whispering, "slow down."

When you feel no joy and life feels heavy, your brain whispers, "You're carrying too much."

When you feel like shutting down or wonder what's wrong with you, your brain is trying to tell you, "You matter too."

> Ignoring the whispers forces them to get louder until you crash.

Ignoring the whispers forces them to get louder until you crash with health problems, fractured relationships, and poor decisions made from exhaustion instead of clarity. But listening to the whispers opens a different path, one marked by alignment, energy, and presence. We can't always prevent what's coming, but we can prepare to meet it with resilience.

Reflection

James Baldwin once said, "Not everything that is faced can be changed, but nothing can be changed until it is faced."

Let's take a moment and face some truth. Ask yourself these questions:

- Have I felt more exhausted than usual lately?
- Have I overreacted to something small?
- Have I noticed myself crying more, or feeling flat and disconnected?
- Is my body trying to get my attention?

Write down one whisper you've been ignoring. Awareness is often the first nudge toward regrouping before burnout takes hold.

Chapter Three

The Limbo Season

Accept it. Change it. Move on.

—Janel Donohue

IF YOU'RE WONDERING if there really can be good stress, think about those in-between times. "What was" has ended, but "what will be" hasn't arrived. This lack of good stress—direction and momentum—can feel unbearable. We search diligently for the next thing. I call this Limbo Season.

Most of us try to rush through these days. But what if the in-between can be more than just a holding pattern? What if it's a sacred space where clarity quietly takes root? What if limbo is not a mistake or a weakness, but rather a purposeful pause that asks you to listen differently?

Jim Rohn wrote in his book *The Seasons of Life* that "you cannot change the seasons, but you can change yourself."[8] His words remind us that just like winter gives way to spring, every season of life has its purpose. Limbo isn't a detour—it's a season in its own right. We can't control how long it lasts, but we can use it to prepare, reflect, and grow so that when the next season comes, we meet it with new strength.

When Fear and Doubt Feel Loud

There's a particular kind of fear that shows up during limbo. We feel isolated and wonder if we've lost our edge. Doubt hovers like a dark cloud, whispering that we're no longer needed. Because our brain doesn't know what's coming next, it tries to protect us by staying on high alert.

Without the familiar cues from the season we just left, everything feels risky. Our nervous system begins to treat everything like a threat.

The limbic system—especially the amygdala—doesn't like ambiguity. Emotional danger feels as threatening as physical danger. Shifting roles, changing identities, or simply not knowing what's next can activate the body's internal "danger alert" loops of anxiety, second-guessing, or shame.

> Sometimes the boldest thing you can do is pause.

The work here isn't to shut fear down. It's to retrain the brain to recognize that fear doesn't always mean stop. Sometimes it means slow down and listen. I love the quote, "Sometimes the boldest thing you can do is pause." You can still move forward with fear. You can question your calling and still remain rooted in it. You can let fear speak without letting it lead. You can give it your attention, not your confidence.

Denis's Story

For years, Denis Gianoutsos traveled the world speaking, facilitating, and coaching executives, leaders, and high performers at the top of their game. He loved every moment of what he did. His voice was his instrument, the tool that allowed him to inspire, challenge, and connect with people across cultures and industries.

One day, everything changed. His voice began to sound hoarse, raspy, and breathy. At first, he blamed fatigue. But when it didn't improve, fear set in.

As the months went on, it became harder to speak. His voice would fade, and at times he struggled to get words out. Frustrated and deeply emotional, he felt like his voice wasn't being heard, neither literally nor figuratively. Not knowing what caused it made it even more frightening.

Questions filled his mind. What if this was permanent? What if he could never speak again? Denis' voice was not just his livelihood; it was part of who he was.

After several tests and anxious months of uncertainty, doctors discovered a tumor on his left vocal cord. In that instant, it seemed as if his life and career had come to a complete stop. The fear of the unknown was overwhelming.

Thankfully, the tumor turned out to be benign. Filled with deep relief and gratitude, he felt as though life had paused and offered him a second chance.

> Slow progress is still progress.

The recovery that followed was slow but steady. But as the saying goes, "Slow progress is still progress."

Denis stayed in his corporate role for another year as he healed, his voice growing stronger each day. But his season of Limbo changed something inside. For more than ten years, he had thought about starting his own business. This experience gave him the courage to finally take that step.

Today, Denis runs the global executive leadership development company, Business is Leading Change Partners, and hosts the Leadership is Changing podcast, which reaches thousands of leaders worldwide. What felt like an ending became a defining moment—a regroup that prepared him for a far more powerful beginning.

Limbo Has Purpose

I once thought limbo meant I was stuck. Looking back, I see how it created space for reshaping. After my mom's death, my caregiving role suddenly expanded, and I felt direction-less. I wasn't the daughter, wife, or mom I had been, and I certainly wasn't who I wanted to be. It felt like failure.

In the silence, I realized Limbo wasn't wasted time. It was unseen growth. My friend, Janel, captured the essence of limbo and uncomfortable change better than any definition could. Her phrase became an anchor for me: "Accept it. Change it. Or Move on."

Acceptance doesn't mean resignation. It's resilience. It's the courage to meet limbo as it is, take what you can from it, and move forward when the time is right. Limbo allowed me to slow down, stay present without forcing the next step, and regroup without guilt. When you hold space for what isn't yet defined, you make room for the truest version of you to emerge.

You don't have to be crystal clear to be brave. You just have to stay present long enough for clarity to catch up.

Reflection

Think about the last time you felt in Limbo. Maybe one chapter of your life ended, but the next hadn't yet begun. Perhaps you experienced a loss that left a space nothing else could fill. Or maybe you or someone you love faced a health challenge that felt overwhelming and unending.

- What fears and doubts rose to the surface during that time?
- What quiet truth or strength began to take shape underneath it all?
- What did that season reveal or teach you?

Limbo often strips away the noise and forces us to face what we've been avoiding. It can become the space where strength deepens, clarity forms, and resilience quietly takes root.

> *Sometimes we live in regret for the times*
> *we didn't listen to ourselves,*
> *but we have the ability to become wiser.*

—Unknown

- If you're standing in that in-between space right now, what quiet truth or strength might you draw from it? Sometimes the season that feels like a pause is actually preparing you for what's next.

Chapter Four

When Life Regroups You—The Reset You Didn't Choose

The oak fought the wind and was broken;
the willow bent when it must and survived.

—Robert Jordan

WE SELDOM CHOOSE the moments that make regrouping most imperative. A crisis, a diagnosis, or a sudden loss can shift everything instantly. Unwelcome interruptions, though painful, almost always carry a need to grieve as well as the counterintuitive mandate to reset.

When loss creates deep heart aches, it's often love speaking in the rawest form. Grief is the measure of how deeply you cared, how fully you let someone or something matter to you. The pain is evidence that your love and connection were real. Seasons of stress and limbo quietly invite us to take a step back and regroup, but these harsh realities stop us in our tracks.

Working Through Grief

After a terminally ill team member died, a client confided, "I don't feel like myself anymore. I'm maxed out and I can't enjoy the work I used to love." Exhausted and running on fumes, he had lost sight of who he was outside the grind.

He wanted clarity around what his life should look like in this season, both personally and professionally. But first, he had to develop self-awareness about how grief can shape how people show up at work and in life.

He revisited his values and explored what made him feel creative and at peace. Small adjustments brought transformation over time. His most impactful discovery was how nature boosted his thinking and creativity. He found that walking outdoors sparked ideas and helped him think more clearly. Nature returned a sense of perspective he had lost.

Research from Stanford echoes my client's experience.[9] They found that walking in nature for just ninety minutes significantly decreased the brain's rumination—those looping, negative thoughts that can lead to burnout and depression. It also improved mood and cognitive function, showing that our brains actually reset more effectively in natural environments than in urban ones.

Working Through Unexpected Setbacks

An unexpected detour for my client gave him more proof—literally.

On a work trip with a major deadline looming, his car broke down in the middle of nowhere. No cell service, no stores, no way to call for help. He had one option—walk four hours to find a phone. His fury and remembering everything that had gone wrong pushed him as he headed toward the phone.

But as he walked, something shifted.

He told me later, "I started thinking about our conversation, and remembered I could either stew in frustration or use the time for something useful. So I started mentally working through the project."

Left with only nature and his own thoughts, he began piecing together the solution to his high-stakes problem. After he got home, he finished his project in record time.

"It was one of the best things I've ever submitted. I don't think I would've come up with those ideas if I had stayed indoors," he said. "Being forced to slow down actually helped me think faster."

We don't plan for this kind of regrouping. They feel inconvenient, uncomfortable, difficult, unfair, or worse. But if we let them, these moments often create something we didn't know we needed.

> Being forced to slow down actually helped me think faster.

Not every opportunity for regroup shows up as a car breaking down. Some arrive quietly and more personal—like the slow, steady stretch of time spent caring for someone else. These seasons seldom feel profound while you're in them; they seem heavy. But over time, they reveal something we were too distracted to see: how often we ignored our own needs because we didn't know how to face our own limits.

Every unexpected crisis has the potential to bring clarity to what's important and help us see what we've been running from. They challenge our plans and shake our confidence. Sometimes the plan gets broken, so you can build something better.

For many, unplanned interruptions bring grief. Some lose loved ones. Others lose a dream, a role, or even a sense of identity. Regardless of the source of the sorrow, it changes you. It forces you to slow down and feel what you've been avoiding.

Let's be real, grief deserves space and attention. It's not something to rush or fix. When honored, grief becomes a teacher. It deepens your empathy and reorganizes your priorities. And often, it reveals a quieter strength you didn't know you had.

Draw the Line in the Sand

That Thanksgiving moment at Cracker Barrel with my dad created immediate feelings of exposure and shame. But those feelings became a line in the sand. I realized I couldn't change the past, but I could change the story going forward.

Shortly after that day, that sinking feeling I had at Cracker Barrel was confirmed. My dad was officially diagnosed with Huntington's disease—a genetic and progressive brain disorder that slowly robs a person of their movement, thinking, and independence. Suddenly, the story was bigger than mere family history. I knew that in order to walk this journey with my father, I had to learn how to take care of myself, including my brain—emotionally, spiritually, and physically.

That's when I came across *Change Your Brain, Change Your Life* by Dr. Daniel Amen. His words shifted how I saw mental health. For the first time, I understood that what I'd

> In order to walk this journey with my father, I had to learn how to take care of myself.

been feeling wasn't just about willpower or mindset—it was about brain health. That single shift gave me language for what I'd felt but couldn't name. It also gave me hope that things could change—for myself and for others.

His work confirmed what I now call REGROUP—small, brain-smart resets that bring me back to center when life starts to feel overwhelming. It's also a lifestyle. It helps me get ahead of the stress, and I'm confident it can help you too.

That unexpected moment at Cracker Barrel became a turning point. It brought buried pain to the surface but also cracked the door open to something new—a more hopeful story about how I could walk this journey with my dad while still living with purpose and meaning. It showed me what could be rebuilt, even in the middle of hard things.

And, in a full-circle way, I never could have predicted that years later I would go on to work for Dr. Amen and help make an impact on others. He's given me permission to share many of the same tools that helped me find my footing. Now, I use those tools—and more—to support leaders, caregivers, and others who carry more than their share. Together, we use practical tools to uncover the signs of being stretched too thin so they find their way back to themselves with a steadier kind of resilience.

We may not be able to control every moment, every crisis, or every diagnosis, but we can choose how we walk through them—lightening the load and tending to the weight we too often carry alone.

Let's REGROUP.

Reflection

Consider these questions. Take time to write your thoughts, even if they're messy. You don't need definitive answers.

Sometimes clarity begins by giving language to what has never been spoken.

- What situation, past or present, still feels heavy to you?
- How has it shaped the way you see yourself or what you believe is possible?
- If you drew a line in the sand, separating your past from your future, how might you begin to change the story going forward—for yourself and others?

Chapter Five

Your Built-In Regroup System

*The moment you change your perception
is the moment you rewrite the chemistry of your body.*

—Dr. Bruce H. Lipton

ON A RECENT trip to Kauai, my family and I planned to take in the breathtaking views of Waimea Canyon—the "Grand Canyon of the Pacific." Unfortunately, fog and rain hid the vista. Later in the week, we tried a different approach—a helicopter ride. From above, we saw sights unavailable from the ground, even on a clear day. That regroup let us experience something bigger than originally anticipated.

Life can be the same way. Circumstances can often block our path. To move forward, we must rise above, circle back, and see things from a new perspective.

Too often, we treat burnout like a finish line we never saw coming. In truth, the unraveling starts long before the crash. Irritability, chronic stress, lower energy, and inner disconnection try to get our attention. Still, we push on—not because we're careless, but because we care.

We've been conditioned to equate slowing down to unreliable or lazy. But what if the opposite is true? What if regrouping demonstrates the utmost courage and responsibility?

Built-In Features

You've probably felt it more than heard it: "Let's pause. Let's get clear. Let's make this sustainable." Our brains can't sustain continuous full-throttle motion. Your body, nervous system, and brain need intentional pauses. Twenty-four-seven fight-or-flight mode will eventually take us down.

Your body follows a natural circadian rhythm, a 24-hour internal clock that regulates your sleep-wake cycle and helps keep your energy, hormones, and mood in balance. Within that daily rhythm, your brain also runs in ultradian cycles—natural 90–120 minute cycles of alertness and rest that occur throughout your day. These cycles are your brain's way of renewing itself. When we push through the natural dips, we exhaust our mental resources. But when we honor these rhythms—even with a short break, breath, or reset—we give our brain the chance to regroup on its own.

> When we honor these rhythms, we give our brain the chance to regroup on its own.

Research by scientists like Nathaniel Kleitman and Ernest Rossi has shown that these rhythms are vital to productivity, focus, and emotional regulation.[10][11] They are, quite literally, how your brain regroups—not through intensity, but through rhythm, not by pushing harder, but by pausing with intention.

This connects deeply with a quote often attributed to Viktor Frankl: "Between stimulus and response, there is a space. In that space is our power to choose our response. In our response lies our growth and our freedom."

That space is where regrouping happens.

It's the pause your brain is designed to make. The breath before a reaction. The reset that lets you lead yourself, not just your tasks. Regrouping helps you find that space again.

Fortunately, you may not need a six-month sabbatical to recalibrate, breathe, and find footing again. Small resets, done consistently, make a profound difference.

While caring for my dad, just as my business was taking off, one of my sons became homebound due to health reasons. The situation frightened everyone.

I didn't want to leave him alone, but I had already started advertising a women's retreat. Strangely enough, not one person signed up. Without realizing it, I had scheduled the retreat for Mother's Day weekend.

Completely discouraged, I vented to my husband, who immediately saw the positive. "What if this week was meant for you?" The beach house I rented for the event would sit empty. Unless. . .

Though my son and my dad needed me, I went. I found it difficult to unwind, but by the end of that week I felt like myself again—energized, clear, and more grounded. That was my first regroup.

From that point on, I made a commitment. Every month, I would step away, even if just for a short time, to reset. Nine years later, I still honor that rhythm. Over time, I've added smaller daily and weekly moments to regroup. Sometimes the tug-of-war tried to keep me from setting aside time, but I've learned I can't keep going at full speed without space to recover.

With each regroup, I discovered strategies that helped me reach a state of greater energy and peace, physically, mentally, emotionally, and spiritually. I paid attention to the small practices that refreshed me and learned from trial and error. I delved into research and gleaned from experts. Eventually, I took everything I learned and turned it into something easy to remember, so I could return to it again and again. That concept became the REGROUP Framework.[IP]

An Overview

The REGROUP acronym doesn't offer shiny tools or quick-fix strategies, and it won't encourage you to optimize yourself to the point of exhaustion. Instead, REGROUP invites us to ask better questions and slow down enough to hear what our lives have been trying to tell us.

Sometimes the clarity and strength we're chasing show up when we stop forcing and start listening. When we quiet the noise and lean in to hear our hearts, we loosen the ties that pull us in every direction and begin to be put back together.

> REGROUP invites us to ask better questions and slow down enough to hear what our lives have been trying to tell us.

Real momentum doesn't live in the hustle; it lives in the steady rhythm of what grounds you, centers you, and calls you forward. Other systems might encourage you to stop your life and start over. REGROUP unleashes the quiet courage to acknowledge what no longer works and the humility to open your heart to something different, even if it's uncomfortable.

Each letter of REGROUP represents a reset principle. They aren't isolated strategies but interconnected rhythms. When one area grows, others often grow stronger too.

But like a double-edged sword, neglecting the principles of REGROUP has the potential for pitfalls. Without them, we quietly risk burnout and misalignment. We must learn to nurture these principles with intention, so they can help us reset our minds, unlock hidden energy, enjoy productive peace, and feel like ourselves again.

The principles of REGROUP can act as a roadmap with checkpoints along the way. They'll become a mirror to reflect where you may be drifting. While we'll dive deeper in the next section, here's a brief overview of the benefits and risks:

R – **Resilience** Starts Within

Benefit: Developing resilience reconnects you to your inner strength and reminds you that you've overcome hard things before. It becomes a quiet, empowering return to your core.

Risk: Neglecting your resilience will make you believe you're not strong enough and that you have to build strength from scratch, leaving you feeling powerless or stuck.

E – **Energy** is Fuel

Benefit: Recognizing this principle helps you become more intentional with your energy. You'll learn what restores and drains energy and how to treat it like a precious resource.

Risk: Neglecting this principle causes you to over-extend, ignore your energy levels, and normalize exhaustion without you even realizing it. Eventually, even small tasks can feel overwhelming.

G – **Guard** Your Margin

Benefit: Guarding your margin lets you create space to breathe and recover. Boundaries, white space, and rest become anchors during unpredictable times.

Risk: Neglecting this principle makes your time and energy vulnerable. Without margin, you lose your ability to stay steady, and burnout creeps in.

R – **Regulate** Your Nervous System

Benefit: Regulating your nervous system shifts your thoughts from survival mode to a calmer, more connected state. Regulation helps you think clearly, feel safer in your body, and respond instead of react.

Risk: Misunderstanding your nervous system puts you in a chronically activated or disconnected state. Everything feels urgent, and your brain can't access calm, rational thoughts. It's exhausting, even if you don't realize it.

O – **Operate** from Alignment

Benefit: When you operate from what is truly meaningful, your choices reflect your values, not just your obligations. This brings peace, confidence, and clarity to your decisions.

Risk: Neglecting this principle means you'll keep saying yes when your heart means no. You live by someone else's values. Over time, it creates internal friction, resentment, and loss of direction.

U – **Update** Your Thinking

Benefit: Updated thinking helps you challenge limiting beliefs and replaces them with thoughts that support healing, growth, and clarity. This is how you create mental freedom.

Risk: Neglected, old patterns and outdated stories run your life. They become invisible barriers to progress and peace.

P – **Prioritize** Brain Health

Benefit: Prioritizing brain health gives your brain the support it needs to make healthy decisions, build relationships, focus, and the energy it needs.

Risk: Overlooking brain health means missing the root of many of your struggles. Everything feels harder—mood, decisions, memory, focus, and relationships.

It's easy to think of regrouping as a quick reset to get you back on track—but that misses the real point. Regrouping is a way of living that gives your brain and body permission to reset before they reach the breaking point. REGROUP helps you build emotional flexibility and endurance and live in alignment with who you want to be in this season of your life.

Create Sustainable Transformation

In the next pages, you'll find brain-friendly practices you can accomplish in just one or two minutes a day. These micro-practices, based on lived experience and science, can help your brain shift out of overwhelm and back into clarity. They include the work of BJ Fogg, author of *Tiny Habits*, who reminds us that sustainable transformation starts small. Real change isn't about doing more—it's about doing what matters, consistently, in ways that fit your life.

Another book, *Think Again,* by Adam Grant, talks about the importance of rethinking—not because we are wrong, but because growth requires questioning assumptions we've held onto for too long—assumptions about who we have to be, how hard we have to push, or whether it's "weak" to pause. [12] The REGROUP Framework invites these questions—not just about your habits, but about your worth, your wiring, and your way forward. REGROUP doesn't ask you to fix yourself. It encourages you to see yourself with more clarity and compassion.

We don't have to chase REGROUP. It was wired into our brains at birth. We just need the key to unlock it.

Up until now, you've been doing your best. But what if pushing harder isn't the only way forward? In fact, it might not even be the wisest. REGROUP encourages you to adjust instead of push. You don't have to rewrite your whole story. You just have to be honest about what's no longer working and allow space for something new.

The REGROUP Framework doesn't want you to lose your fire. It simply wants to teach you how to protect your flame.

Reflection

From this point on, our reflection will encompass three key aspects: Pause, Reflect, and Regroup. Take a minute to consider these questions.

Pause—Where do you move on autopilot even though your brain and body are asking for a reset?

Reflect—Which part of the REGROUP Framework do you feel most connected to already, and which part is quietly calling for your attention?

Regroup—Take a two-minute reset to create your first small shift–breathe deep, set a boundary, or take a moment to rethink your need to push through. Consider experimenting with box breathing or the 4-7-8 breathing method. (Though, take care when driving. Some people get lightheaded the first time they try this.)

Box breathing follows this breathing pattern:

- Breathe in for four seconds
- Hold the breath for four seconds
- Breathe out for four seconds
- Hold the breath for four seconds

In the 4-7-8 breathing method, you:

- Breathe in for four seconds
- Hold the breath for seven seconds
- Breathe out for eight seconds

As we move into the REGROUP Framework, these practices will give you a head start on learning to support your brain's natural rhythm.

PART 2

REGROUP

Chapter Six

Resilience Starts Within

Strength is found in memories, not merely moments.[IP]

—Barbara Gustavson

EVERYONE HAS A flame within. Sometimes it burns brightly, and at other times, it feels like life is trying to snuff it out. That's why we need resilience.

The first "R" in our framework becomes crucial when we feel our fire diminishing. Like the flame on an oil lamp, too much wick burns through our fuel supply. But when we manage the wick and protect our fuel, the flame can light the room for hours.

When you sense your inner flame flickering, resilience steadies it. It's not something you build from scratch; it's something deep inside you can build upon. Resilience is woven into your brain's natural capacity to adapt, recalibrate, and recover. But when you've been in survival mode, stuck in overdrive, or running on fumes, it's easy to forget it's there.

Your strength hasn't left you. It needs to be remembered and awakened.

Resilience Lives in Your Memory—Not Just Your Muscles

In the movie *The Lion King*, Mufasa tells Simba, "Remember who you are." The young king hadn't lost his title or his abilities. He didn't need to become something new. He simply needed to return to who he always had been.

Resilience resurfaces when we remember where we've been. Each of us has already faced many difficult things. Some were obvious. Others, no one saw except you. Either way, somehow you've made it through 100 percent of your hardest days so far. I like Will Packer's quote, "Take the hardest thing that's ever happened to you and take more from it than it took from you." We don't always see the enormous strength we've demonstrated until we step back and see ourselves in the bigger picture. It's easy to see only what's in the moment.

When we talk about resilience, most envision a rubber band stretched to its fullest yet able to snap back into position. But true resilience isn't always about stretching further; it's also about knowing the limits of your elasticity. When we operate within what Dr. Dan Siegel calls our "window of tolerance," or our resilience zone, our brain and nervous system can process stress and still function with clarity and intention.[13] Outside that window of capacity, we get overstretched. We feel revved up—anxious, irritable, or overstimulated—or we shut down—disconnected, foggy, or numb. These aren't signs of weakness. Your nervous system is communicating that something is off.

To keep from breaking, our system is designed to take small pauses—moments of breath, reflection, or movement—that allow us to re-enter our resilience zone where our thinking is clearer, our emotions steadier, and our energy more aligned.

What Shapes Our Resilience

Resilience isn't just a mindset. It's also shaped by our nervous system, which develops patterns based on our experiences and the meanings we attach to them. The level of safety, support, and stability we had growing up plays a big role in how our resilience develops.

The ACEs (Adverse Childhood Experiences) study revealed that early trauma and stress affects brain development and shapes how we cope as adults. People with higher ACE scores tend to struggle more with stress and emotional regulation, not because they're weak but because of the way their systems adapted for survival.[14]

Some of our capacity to "bounce back" has been shaped by trauma, which can leave deep imprints that need careful unpacking. That kind of deep healing often requires safe spaces and skilled professional support. If that's where you are, reach out to a qualified and trusted practitioner for guidance.

> Growth takes place when you're challenged, not comfortable.

Regardless of what has shaped you, you've already learned to adapt and grow strong through lived experience. Someone once said, "Growth takes place when you're challenged, not comfortable."[15] You might not call it resilience at the time, but every pause, every boundary, every small shift you made has been strengthening this essential REGROUP principle.

Resilience Is Built Through Real Life, Not Perfect Conditions

Psychologists Richard Tedeschi and Lawrence Calhoun studied what they called Post-Traumatic Growth—the idea that adversity can lead to transformation in five key areas:

- A deeper appreciation for life
- Stronger, more meaningful relationships
- A sense of personal strength
- A reordering of priorities
- A greater sense of meaning or spiritual depth

Growth doesn't erase pain, but they can coexist. War veterans who get together and share their stories with purpose find strength in the pain. Remembering the transformation we've experienced through difficulties reinforces the fact that good things can take root in the aftermath of disruption, and the way we respond matters.

In my first book, *Permission to Be Bold*, I shared a story about Biosphere 2, a sealed ecological dome where trees grew quickly but collapsed before reaching maturity. Without the resistance of the wind, they never grew strong. Trees need storms to send out sturdy roots and develop flexible trunks.

Resilience develops the same way—not from ease, but from engagement. From learning to bend without breaking and growing through life's friction.

You Can Build Resilience—At Any Age

The good news is our brains can be retrained. Neuroplasticity gives us the ability to rewire how we respond to stress. You don't need to stay stuck. No matter where you begin, new patterns can be built that support you now.

Adolf Meyer introduced the idea of neuroplasticity in the 1890s; however, until the 1970s, most scientists ridiculed his theories. Today, we know every pause, reflection, and response can create new pathways of recovery and clarity. The changes and growth that science once believed could only happen in the brain of a toddler have been proven to happen throughout a lifetime.[16]

> Each new action or mindset shift retrains our brain.

That's how we build resilience. Each new action or mindset shift retrains our brain. Every time we survive a situation, we rewire. This is the core of the REGROUP Framework—small shifts that build strength over time.

Bonnie St. John calls this *micro-resilience*: reclaiming energy and focus through small, intentional resets that add up to lasting strength.

I had the privilege of meeting and interviewing Bonnie, and her story is a powerful example of resilience in action. Despite losing her leg at the age of five, she went on to become a Paralympic medalist, a Rhodes Scholar, and a White House advisor.[17] She embodies what it means to keep getting back up, one small reset at a time.

Just like circling the island of Kauai gave me a new perspective, we build resilience when we look above the fog of fear and fatigue. From the ground, we see obstacles. From above, we see options. That's what the REGROUP journey is about. So let me ask: Are you ready for the mental helicopter ride?

Reflection

> *Real resilience knows when to take a step back.*
>
> —Unknown

Pause—Slow down for a moment to consider the statement: Strength is found in memories, not merely in moments. When was the last time you reminded yourself of something hard you've overcome and came out stronger?

Reflect—Write down some of the ways you've been strong in the past. Nothing is too small; everything has shaped your resilience.

Regroup—If you're going through a difficult situation currently, take ten minutes to be still, and use your list to remind yourself you are strong.

Chapter Seven

Energy Is Fuel

Energy is precious and limited; we must optimize it.[IP]

—Barbara Gustavson

YOU MIGHT FIND yourself mentally exhausted and can't figure out why. It's not just you, it's an epidemic.

From responsibilities and perfectionism to emotional overfunctioning, so much of what drains us comes from circumstances out of our control or habits and expectations we've carried far too long. Imagine how much would shift if you could identify what drains you and guard your energy with intention. One of the hardest lessons I've had to learn is that not everything that demands your attention deserves it.

Identify Your Energy Drains

When oil lamps were the primary source of light, no one intentionally let the fire burn out. Refueling in the dark was difficult. Instead, our ancestors watched for the signs of a failing flame. Keeping the flame high for too long used extra fuel, and they kept that in mind as they read by the lantern light.

It's the same with our energy. Most of us begin with good intentions, but when we overextend ourselves without noticing the warning signs, life siphons our fuel until we're running on fumes.

I started to see this more clearly when I noticed where I was "**overing**"—overdoing, overthinking, overcommitting. That little word *over*. It means *too much* or *beyond what's manageable.* It's the point where something spills past its natural limit.

I'm sure you'll recognize these common "overs."

1. **Overwhelming** doesn't always come from doing too much. It often happens when we're carrying or caring too much. This is especially common for those who support others. Caring itself isn't the problem. But when we over-help—either by trying to control outcomes or not allowing others to help carry the load—it becomes the metaphorical candle burning at both ends. It drains us faster than we can refuel, leaving us with unnecessarily depleted energy reserves.

2. **Overthinking** can disguise itself as caring or trying to fix things. It often looks like replaying conversations, second-guessing decisions, or trying to plan for every possible outcome. What feels like "being responsible" can actually keep us stuck in mental loops that exhaust us.

3. **Overworrying** happens when healthy love, responsibility, and preparation move into the world of "what-ifs." A little worry can help us make wise decisions, but when it grows into fear or doubt, it steals today's peace.

4. **Overcommitting** often shows up as saying yes when we should say no. When we commit from a place of

genuine care, our flame lights the path for others. But when we commit to avoiding disappointing people, we silently let ourselves down.

5. **Overworking** can look admirable, and some workplaces reward it. But if exhaustion becomes your proof of worth, the cost is too high.

6. **Overgiving** occurs when we try to pour from an empty cup and call it compassion.

Refueling, Protecting, Conserving

We've been conditioned to treat our energy like it's endless—to spend it freely and prove our worth by how much of it we give away. We admire people who make it through the "overs."

But here's the truth—your energy is finite. We need to embrace the quote, "Energy is currency. Spend it where it matters." This precious resource, like fuel, electricity, or clean water, needs to be protected, replenished, and cherished. Consider how the world treats energy sources. We've designed systems around conserving them. No one ever shamed an oil lamp for needing more fuel.

Why then, do we override and overextend and wonder why we're foggy, frustrated, or flattened? Burnout does not prove you care more.

> Energy is currency. Spend it where it matters.

This isn't about time management or productivity. It's about **energy stewardship**, learning to recognize what drains you, what restores you, and how to protect your reserves like they matter—because they do. By pausing, reflecting, and regrouping, you can replenish your energy supply. These few practices make excellent tools for refueling:

- Create white space in your schedule
- Say no without explanation
- Have a conversation with someone who sees you clearly
- Take walks, exercise, dance, or move in some other way that restores rather than depletes
- Remind yourself you don't have to fix everything

We have to learn to protect our energy day to day. It's not always the workload that depletes us; it's the hidden "overing" that drains our supplies. I don't know who said it, but the saying is true: "You can aim high without running on empty."

Your oil lamp needs fuel to illuminate the space around it. Empty equals burnout. We need to refuel early, often, and on purpose. REGROUP creates a practice of returning to center when life yanks you off track.

It's Not the Doing—It's the "Overing"[IP]

Before we dive further into refueling, I want to be clear: REGROUP does not replace medical guidance. If you're constantly feeling exhausted, foggy, or "not yourself," it's wise to check in with a trusted health provider. Sometimes what we think is stress or "being tired" is actually our body asking for deeper support. It invites us to address nutrient deficiencies, hormone imbalances, chronic inflammation, or other conditions that need care.

Fortunately, you can seek medical care and REGROUP. This framework isn't either/or. The framework will help you tune in, notice patterns, and honor the messages your body and brain send.

Every bit of "overing" begins with good intentions. Left unchecked, good quietly shifts from strength to strain, from doing to overdoing. Anyone who feels called to serve, lead, or carry more than most can become susceptible to it. We start to believe that more effort is the answer. We don't see it's really the beginning of an energy leak.

> You're not lazy.
> You're likely
> depleted.

When your command center becomes overloaded or overstretched, everything suffers. You start to feel it in your thinking, mood, memory, decisions, and emotional regulation. You end up not wanting to do anything, but you're not lazy. You're likely depleted. When that happens, it's time to identify your drains. What is stealing your energy or blowing out your flame?

Reflection

Pause—Identify your energy drains. Not all energy drains are easily seen. We each have habits, thoughts, roles, or relationships that consistently leave us feeling depleted—even if they're masked as "doing the right thing."

List your physical, mental, emotional, social, and spiritual energy drains.

Circle the ones that potentially come from overings.

Reflect—Now that you've identified our energy drains, it's time to name the things that refuel you. These aren't things that make you feel good for a moment. Your energy builders include the people, practices, or rhythms that actively strengthen your capacity—mentally, emotionally, or physically. For example:

To discover your personal energy builders, ask yourself:

- Who or what helps me come back to myself?
- Who or what expands my clarity or steadiness?
- Who or what helps me function from fullness instead of force?

Regroup—Regrouping invites you to make one small shift that could become a regular part of your life. This shift will help you refuel and protect your energy.

Complete this sentence, putting your most obvious "overing" in the first blank and your favorite way to refuel in the second.:

Instead of _____, I will choose _____.

Chapter Eight

Guard Your Margin

Healthy people have healthy boundaries.

—Barbara Gustavson

HOW DO YOU feel when you are in a large crowd with people pushing against you? We put up with it at football games and celebrity concerts, but, truth be told, we prefer to leave a seat between us and the next person if we can. Everyone likes that buffer zone, a little space where we can breathe.

When you're caring for others, you need that same kind of gap in your life. Like white space on the edge of our paper, we need margins to keep the chaos at bay, a line that sets limits. And while our lives might not ever be as neat and tidy as the straight line on the left side of our notebook, knowing where the line is can make a huge difference in our Regroup.

Guarding your margin doesn't happen without intention. We have to create that boundary and then fiercely protect it. Guarding your margin gives you breathing room, allowing you to stay steady, clear, and available to show up for what matters most. Without the guard, your flame burns just bright enough for everyone to see. No one but you realizes it's on the verge of burning out.

Many helpers, caregivers, and high-capacity leaders live with their flame on a constant high. They don't understand the quote, "Doing less doesn't mean you're becoming less." Giving everything, they never create support systems that allow them to step back. It appears selfless, but without boundaries, their unstable efforts consume their entire fuel supply. Over time, you can't rescue anyone; you and the one you're caring for both fall.

My Wake-Up Call

I lived three and a half hours away from my parents when my mom passed. Still, in addition to my daily commute to work—almost two hours in the opposite direction—raising two boys with my husband, and teaching piano on week-ends, I managed my dad's care. I said "yes" to almost every request. Rest could wait—or so I told myself.

Even through the burnout, I tried to do everything for everyone. With my fuel supply depleted, I needed help navigating caregiving decisions, so I reached out for support with someone who specialized in elder care. Her advice landed like a jolt. "The problem isn't your dad. The problem is you have no boundaries."

She was right. I had no margin, no breathing room. Resentful and running on fumes, I experienced regular panic attacks behind closed doors and felt ashamed of my feelings.

I needed to find a way to clear my mind and replenish my energy. My calendar didn't allow for immediate changes, and a sabbatical was out of the question. So, I started simple. I gave myself five minutes of uninterrupted peace each day. It sounds laughably small, but those five minutes cracked a wall I didn't realize I'd built. Over time, that tiny pocket of space helped restore clarity, decision-making, and compassion for myself and others.

Boundaries: The Guardrails of Margin

Margin isn't laziness or self-indulgence. It's the breathing room and white space we all need in between all the things we're doing. In brain terms, breathing room in your packed schedule gives your prefrontal cortex—the part of your brain responsible for planning, decision-making, and emotional regulation—a chance to function at its best.[18]

> Margin gives us room to pause before responding.

Without this white space, our nervous system responds, and our brains shift into chronic reactive mode. We become quick to snap, slow to think, and more likely to make decisions we regret. Margin gives us room to pause before responding, to think before deciding, and to show up fully.

In *Boundaries for Leaders*, Henry Cloud describes boundaries as structures that protect your focus and filter out what doesn't serve you.[19] Rather than walls to keep people out, boundaries are guardrails to keep you intact.

> Saying no is a strategy, not a shortcoming.

Boundaries are simply decisions made in advance about what you will and won't allow. It's embracing the quote, "Saying no is a strategy, not a shortcoming."[1P] Margins protect your energy and attention so you can sustain your calling without erasing yourself in the process.

Guarding our margins also means we protect our time. One of my boundaries is to block off non-negotiable white space in my calendar. Whether it's minutes between meetings or an hour in the afternoon, each calendar entry creates a margin that protects my flame.

Setting boundaries teaches your brain that you can protect your peace.

Research consistently links clear boundaries with better mental health, lower stress, and increased resilience.[20] When work-life boundaries blur, emotional exhaustion spikes unless people intentionally maintain restorative habits like adequate sleep and regular movement.[21]

Boundaries aren't just psychological—they're physiological. Protecting our margins helps regulate cortisol levels, supports immune function, and preserves cognitive performance under stress.[22]

Because we're not running on fumes and we've learned how to refuel before we hit empty, we recover faster from stress. As one of my mentors often reminded me when I was caring for my mom and dad: *Do what you reasonably can—and let the rest go.* It sounds simple, but for people who care deeply and overdo it when it comes to supporting others, it's the hardest discipline of all. And it's the foundation of a life that can sustain you during difficult seasons.

Reflection

Pause—One of the fastest ways to see where you need a boundary is to examine what you've been tolerating. Because some seem small, we don't think about how much energy they consume. Here are a few common ones:

- Saying yes to meetings or people that drain you

- Eating lunch at your desk every day
- Living with clutter that keeps you distracted
- Being the default problem-solver for every "urgent" situation

Now, put this book down, grab a sheet of paper, and write down ten things that you've been tolerating—big or small—and letting subtly steal your energy without realizing it. The more you tolerate, the more your margin erodes.

Reflect—You may be tempted to overhaul your boundaries overnight, but that usually backfires. Small, consistent changes will set you up for success. Try creating one new non-negotiable weekly. Here are a few ideas:

- Take five minutes of "no-interruption" reset time each afternoon.
- No phone calls after 7:00 p.m. unless it's a true emergency.
- Say, "Let me check my calendar" before committing to anything.

Every time you follow through, you strengthen neural pathways linked to self-respect and self-protection.[23]

Regroup—Choose one small boundary this week to create space for margin. Add it to your calendar, and protect it like you would a meeting with your most important client. Then, notice what shifts; not just in your schedule, but in your clarity, energy, and presence. Don't forget to come back to this place each week and set a new boundary until you feel like your flame has been adequately protected. Guarding your margin isn't selfish. It's how you stay steady when you're walking on the edge.

Chapter Nine

Regulate Your Nervous System

Staying present creates productive peace.[IP]

—Barbara Gustavson

WHEN WE'RE LEADING, caring, and pressed on every side, we typically don't think about our nervous system. We push forward and force ourselves to focus through the fog. *Hold it together,* our inner selves whisper over and over. Somewhere between hyper-alert and emotional shutdown, we keep going because we're strong and we know how to get things done. All the while, our bodies crave energy to keep our flame burning bright.

Productive Peace

Regulation lets us tune in and learn the natural rhythm of our nervous system. It recognizes when our flame burns too high or dips too low and supports our nervous system so we can stay steady, present, and connected. Regulating our nervous system creates Productive Peace.

Everyone wants peace—that state of safety and steadiness in your body and mind, even in the midst of chaos. Productive peace goes one step further. It puts us in that place of grounded awareness and combines it with purpose. More than a quiet space of meditation, productive peace gives us mental clarity, emotional steadiness, and grounded presence that allows us to think clearly, relate well, and respond wisely even when life becomes challenging. Our relationships benefit, our creativity grows, it enhances our problem-solving, and our goals feel more achievable.

Healthy Versus Unhealthy Nervous System Responses

Your nervous system has two main responses to stress: the Sympathetic and the Parasympathetic systems. The former acts as your body's accelerator; you might know it as the fight-or-flight response. While the second becomes your body's brake, encouraging you to rest and digest.

> More than a quiet space of meditation, productive peace gives us mental clarity, emotional steadiness, and grounded presence.

A healthy nervous system moves fluidly between the two. We rise to meet a challenge, then return to baseline. With a regulated nervous system, after we speak up in a tense meeting, we quickly relax. We can comfort a distressed friend and sleep soundly that night. Our hearts race before a presentation, but afterward we laugh with colleagues.

An unhealthy nervous system response happens when our bodies react without processing the situation. We get stuck in activation (hyperarousal) or shutdown (hypoarousal). Rather than character flaws, these are signs your nervous system is out of rhythm.

Hyperarousal, or activation can show up as:	Hypoarousal, or shutdown, can show up as:
Constant irritability	Emotional numbness
Trouble sleeping	Lack of motivation
Overanalyzing every detail	Foggy thinking
Feeling like everything is urgent	Disconnection from others

Dr. Stephen Porges developed the Polyvagal Theory to explain the way the vagus nerve contributes to the parasympathetic mode. The vagus nerve—the longest cranial nerve—connects your brain to your body and plays a major role in regulating heart rate, digestion, and emotional state. A well-toned vagus nerve supports calm, connection, and resilience.[24]

When we don't feel safe, our bodies move into Sympathetic Mode. Whether the danger is psychological or physical, when a situation begins to feel unsafe, our nervous system sends hormones to our heart, lungs, arms, and legs when a situation begins to feel unsafe to activate us for survival. Our body focuses on protection, not progress. In a dysregulated system, we might react without thinking and not be able to move past the event. In a regulated system, we respond appropriately, and when the threat passes, the Ventral Branch of the vagus nerve moves us into a healthy Parasympathetic mode. We can rest and relax. Stress lowers, and we return to calm.

On the other hand, when the vagus nerve isn't in its healthy state, the other branch takes over. When we should be in Sympathetic mode, the Dorsal Branch of the vagus nerve triggers the freeze response. In a dangerous situation, instead of going into survival mode, our vital organs slow down, and we become immobile. When this state causes us to withdraw, it can prove harmful. We need connection, and it's easy for an unhealthy nervous system to send some personalities into dangerous, lonely places without them ever realizing.[25] The key to regulation is learning how to activate the Ventral Vagal State so we can quickly return to a space where we can think clearly, connect better, and recover faster.

The Power of Co-Regulation

One of the powerful benefits of connection is the part it plays in co-regulation. Co-regulation happens when another person—or even an animal—helps your nervous system return to balance.

I love the way horses participate in co-regulation. I once worked with an equine program at a farm that supported first responders, healthcare workers, and veterans carrying the invisible weight of Post Traumatic Stress Disorder (PTSD). Some of the participants came to us after traditional therapy hadn't brought the relief they needed, and many were holding on by a thread in their personal or professional lives.

Horses have nervous systems that are constantly on guard. Being prey animals, meaning other animals prey on them, horses are wired for survival. They are astonishingly perceptive and can pick up other animals' and humans' nervous systems. When someone approaches them with tension or guardedness, the horse senses it and mirrors and responds with restlessness. When that same person slows their breathing and grounds themselves, the horse often responds with calm.

The six-week equine program begins with resiliency training and learning how to be present. Each session builds on the previous, moving from creating a safe space to managing stress responses, building communication and connection, and finally practicing peace.

Because the horses give immediate feedback, they show participants how easily sounds, smells, or things they see trigger their nervous systems. When they stop to focus on more peaceful memories, the participants calm, and the horse responds within minutes. This awareness allows participants to use their breath and intentional focus to steady themselves. Week after week, the horse honestly mirrored the front-line workers' nervous systems.

By the end of the program, many spoke of life-changing outcomes. One firefighter shared how the breathing technique he practiced with his horse carried him through chaotic emergency situations. A veteran admitted he came in skeptical but left with tools he started to use every day with his family. Another participant recognized how much his stress spilled into his relationships at home, empowering him to change those dynamics. They learned the value of Bob Burg's mantra, "Let Calm be your default."

> Let Calm be your default.

This program opened my eyes to how much we carry beneath the surface. For instance, as a child, I learned to constantly be on guard when my dad was in a high state of anxiety. I carried that constant vigilance into my adult relationships and developed a pattern of overhelping, keeping the peace, and enabling. Awareness allowed me to break these patterns and choose and develop new responses.

Many people have unseen pain and pressure. Fortunately, unhealthy patterns can be changed, but first, we have to recognize them and then be willing to learn new ways to interact. The equine program helped me see the resilience that emerges when people have the space to regulate, connect, and rebuild.

The Regulated Leader

Some of the most effective leaders aren't the loudest or the fastest—they're the most regulated. A regulated leader is grounded enough to pause before reacting, calm enough to think clearly under stress, and humble enough to stay connected even in conflict. Their nervous system sets the emotional tone for everyone around them.

When they're centered, others feel safe. When they're scattered, everyone feels it—especially in moments of crisis.

Regulation doesn't mean suppressing emotion; it means having the awareness and tools to guide your own state so you can guide others well. This is the heart of grounded strength: power that stays steady and clear when everything else feels uncertain. In a crisis, this kind of strength creates trust, steadiness, and a sense of safety that others can anchor to.

Tools to Regulate Your Nervous System

Fortunately, there are a variety of ways to support your nervous system and restore healthy patterns.

1. **Mindfulness**—The first step in regulation is learning to pay attention to your emotions. When you can name your emotion with accuracy, it opens the door

to exploring your feelings and choosing your next step. For example, rather than expressing the broad, "I'm stressed," you recognize, "I'm anxious about this deadline." This acknowledgment lets you pause and become curious, "What does my feeling tell me I need right now?" Being mindful of your nervous system reduces stress reactivity.[26] It also empowers you to step in confidence as you move forward.

2. **Music**—Listening to calming music can lower heart rate and cortisol levels.[27]

3. **Nature**—Spending just twenty minutes outdoors can lower stress hormones.[28]

4. **Writing/Journaling**—Expressive writing can improve mood and reduce intrusive thoughts.[29] Often, we push our emotions down or pretend they're not there. Journaling can give us permission to feel what's present, even when it's uncomfortable. When we acknowledge our feelings, our nervous system can process them rather than fight them. Ignored emotions build pressure, but accepted emotions lose their grip. This kind of acceptance isn't weakness; it's what creates space to understand how we can have a better response instead of reacting on impulse.

5. **Visualization**—Positive imagery can activate the parasympathetic nervous system.[30]

6. **Connection**—Talking with someone you trust can lower stress responses.[31]

These tools open the door for retraining your nervous system. They increase your nervous system's capacity—not just to feel calmer, but also to choose your responses instead of defaulting to old patterns. Regulation creates room for what psychologist Susan David calls *emotional agility*:

"being aware of your emotions, accepting them, and moving forward in a way that aligns with your values."[32]

Regulation creates room for emotional agility.

Think of regulation as steadying the ground beneath your feet, even when life is chaotic, so emotional agility has the flexibility to choose your path. Without regulation, emotions can hit like tidal waves. They either sweep you into quick reactions or pull you into shutdown. Emotional agility lets you surf those waves instead of being knocked down by them.

Regulation and emotional agility working together stop the outbursts that come when you're ruled by your emotions or the shutdown that comes when those emotions feel too overwhelming to express. Your regulated nervous system keeps you steady and helps you stay focused and handle what's in front of you.

Regulation Is a Practice, Not a One-Time Fix

Your nervous system didn't become dysregulated overnight, and it won't reset instantly. Small, consistent habits you can keep up with even in busy seasons will be pivotal for a successful REGROUP. Like shielding a candle from a threatening breeze, these tools will protect your flame, and the more you use them, the more natural they'll become.

I'm still learning too. I need reminders and support just like anyone else. By consistently returning to these tools, I more easily stay grounded. Over time, they stop feeling like effort and start becoming healthy habits.

A classmate in my graduate program shared something that stayed with me and touches me deeply. After hearing my presentation on caregiver emotion regulation, she told me how much it resonated because her husband had been her caregiver through a double lung transplant. She had seen firsthand how a caregiver's emotional state impacts both the giver and receiver of care. What struck her most was how strategies like mindfulness can help buffer stress, while suppressing emotions often backfires. Her words reminded me that regulation isn't theoretical—it shapes real lives, real relationships, and the way we experience moments of both fragility and strength.

Regulation teaches us to pause for a full breath before we respond. We start to notice the benefits when our shoulders drop, even as we hold the tension of a hard decision. It communicates to our body, "Stop running on adrenaline and start leading from alignment."

> Regulation is not indulgent—it's how we're designed.

Regulation doesn't make everything perfect. It gives us peace that *produces.*

Productive peace:

- strengthens in our presence
- brings clarity in our thinking
- adds accuracy to our work
- deepens our relationships

Regulation is not indulgent—it's how we're designed.[IP]

Reflection

Pause—Next time you feel overwhelmed, pay attention to the physical signs you notice first—tight shoulders, faster breathing, racing thoughts, or something else.

Reflect—The mirror of the equine program helps many front-line individuals physically see their inner state. You have a similar mirror. Your body gives honest feedback. It doesn't lie. When your nervous system is dysregulated, it shows up in your posture, your tone, and the way people respond to you. How do you usually feel when you're not regulated? How might others react to your energy? Write down any patterns you've noticed. Even small details can reveal where your stress lives.

Regroup—When we learn to pause, breathe, and regulate, we give ourselves and others the gift of safety. What one regulation tool can you reach for the next time a difficult situation occurs?

Regulation is not a soft skill; it's a necessary survival skill. But beyond survival, it's what helps you think clearly, make better decisions, and lead without running on empty. Regulation is where *productive peace* lives. When your nervous system is regulated, you can stay grounded no matter what's happening around you. That steadiness fuels productive peace, and productive peace fuels your flame, creating a life you can sustain.

Chapter Ten

Operate from Alignment

Your actions tell the world what you value.[IP]

—Barbara Gustavson

I DIDN'T FULLY understand alignment until my own body forced me to pay attention. For months, I had been dealing with unexplained health issues—brain fog, aches, fatigue, and tension that no amount of rest or healthy eating seemed to fix. Eventually, I learned my physical body was literally out of alignment. My upper spine had shifted just enough to disrupt everything else.

When I left the chiropractor's office after my first visit, I felt more relief than I knew I needed. Over the decades, my body had adjusted to the discomfort and dismissed it as just getting older. My body had apparently been waving a red flag, and I let living misaligned become normal.

That experience became a mirror for my inner life. Just like my physical body, the most important areas of my life had slowly shifted out of alignment.

Five Areas of Misalignment

Looking back, I can see the five areas where I was most off track:

- **Purpose**—I lost sight of what gave me joy and meaning.
- **Thinking**—Fear and doubt constantly dictated my actions and inaction, shaping how I viewed myself.
- **Relationships**—I said yes to requests too often, which meant I had to say no to the people that mattered to me, and I rarely asked for help.
- **Emotions**—Although I appeared calm, internally I felt reactive, swinging between exhaustion and frustration.
- **Impact**—I wanted to make a difference, but exhaustion left me with little to give to the people and areas I felt most called to help.

Things began to realign internally when I gained clarity on three anchor points: my purpose, my values, and my energy capacity. When these three priorities came into focus, the rest followed. I reclaimed my identity. My thinking steadied. My relationships deepened. My emotions leveled out. And my impact grew stronger, because it came from alignment, not depletion.

For years, I believed I needed a perfectly crafted purpose statement because well-meaning books and mentors said I should. But the more I tried to make it clear and polished, the less it felt true to me. As someone who's wrestled with perfection, that kind of striving only left me feeling stuck. Eventually, I stopped trying to define it so neatly and started paying attention to what actually gave my life meaning.

For me, that looked like collaborating, coaching, and helping others. These aren't just things I do—they're the places where I come alive. My purpose didn't need a single, perfect sentence. It was already woven into what I was doing every day. I just needed to recognize it and allow that to be enough.

> My purpose was already woven into what I was doing every day.

At the heart of it all, I love guiding people to honor themselves and their strengths while making a difference in the lives of others. There's something powerful about seeing someone step into their own potential and watching that strength ripple outward. That's purpose in motion.

I once had the privilege of interviewing my friend Tom Furness, known as the "Grandfather of Virtual Reality." I asked him how he managed to keep his spark for his vision and calling alive after so many years. He said it's normal for our fire to wane—life gets busy, challenges wear us down, and passion can flicker. But he reminded me that the spark is never gone. It's our responsibility to notice when the flame dims and to do what it takes to reignite it.

Next, I had to reconnect to my values. These give me boundaries. My top values are restoration, peace, learning, developing others, and connectedness. Naming those values gave me a filter. If something doesn't line up with them, I have permission to say no.

The third point of the anchor is the same as the second letter of REGROUP. Your body has a fuel gauge, and it's essential to pay attention to it. We don't have unlimited capacity, no matter how much we wish otherwise. I had to accept that I couldn't say yes to everything and still be true to myself. I don't have the same energy reserves as some people, and that's okay. Protecting my energy meant recognizing that rest and margin weren't signs of weakness—they were part of staying aligned with who I am and how I function best.

From Friction to Freedom

Operating from alignment is more than knowing what matters; it's living what matters, saying yes to what reflects your values and saying no to what pulls you away from who you are. Alignment becomes the anchor that holds you steady. This isn't about rigidity; it's about intentionality.

Misalignment initially creates quiet friction—you say yes to things you regret and no to the passions of your heart. The constant tug-of-war between what you say you want and how you actually live creates turbulence in your life. Alignment doesn't mean perfection; it means rhythm and requires continual tracking. It's the ongoing practice of catching yourself when you drift and gently returning to center.

Four Circles of Alignment

Drawing on decades of clinical work and research, my colleague, Dr. Daniel Amen, and his team teach that a person's brain health is best understood through four key areas. True alignment touches all four.

- **The Biological Circle**—This includes the physical aspects of your brain and the way it works with your body. Genetics, trauma, and many other things either feed or deplete your body and brain's energy and function.

- **The Psychological Circle**—How do you talk to yourself? How do you see yourself? Your thoughts clarify or cloud what matters.

- **The Social Circle**—We each have a variety of connections. Are these healthy or harmful? Your choices shape the health of your closest relationships.

- **The Spiritual Circle**—We are more than our cells, thoughts, and connections. Your alignment grounds you in meaning and direction.

When any one circle is ignored, misalignment seeps in. Neglecting my biological health eventually disrupted the other circles. For some, saying yes at work erodes important relationships and blocks opportunities to fulfill their Spiritual Circle. Others ignore their inner life until even small setbacks feel unbearable.

> Ask yourself,
> "Do my habits and behaviors get me what I want?"
> - Dr. Amen

Dr. Amen created a tool I frequently use with myself and my clients called the One-Page Miracle, based on the four circles above. On a single page, write down what you want in each of the four key circles, then ask Dr. Amen's question, "Do my habits and behavior get me what I want?"[33]

This wasn't easy the first time I completed this exercise. What I wanted:

- For my Biological Circle: I wanted to be physically fit, but my habit of being too sedentary during the day wasn't supporting what I wanted.

- For my Psychological Circle: I wanted to feel more self-love, but my habit of putting myself down didn't match.

- For my Social Circle: I wanted to have more local friends, but because I am more of an introvert, I spent too much time in isolation.

- For my Spiritual Circle: I wanted to have a closer connection with God, but because I was struggling with deep resentment toward past hurts, it kept me from feeling connected to God and my purpose.

"One-Page Miracle" might sound like a big and dramatic promise. That's what I thought when I saw it. But over time, I discovered the power of something much quieter: the tiny miracles—the shift in perspective, a single step forward, or a small change in behavior that compounds over time. Miracles take many forms. For some, it might be an improved bloodwork report after months of effort. For me, it was realizing how one small shift could ripple into positive changes in my focus, relationships, and energy.

Many people believe transformation requires a complete life overhaul. But often, it's just one tiny step, a single clear choice, one yes or one no that begins to shift everything. What about you—what small step could bring you closer to alignment in those four circles? What small change could make a big difference and feel like your own little miracle?

> Your next level won't come from hustle, it'll come from alignment.

As Allison Michels says, "Your next level won't come from hustle, it'll come from alignment."

Jarvis's Story

Jarvis Bailey, a pastor, author, and teacher, walked through a difficult season. On the outside, he kept going, but underneath, he carried heavy responsibilities and unresolved pain from past trauma. Eventually, he reached the end of his capacity. Exhausted and overwhelmed, with no answers left, he knew he needed to regroup.

The shift came not from sheer willpower but in his daily time with God. In those quiet moments of reading scripture, praying, and seeking guidance, Jarvis felt a renewed sense of strength and connection. The trials that nearly broke him realigned his priorities and anchored him to a verse that continues to inspire him: James 1:2-4. "Consider it pure joy, my brothers and sisters, whenever you face trials of many kinds, because you know that the testing of your faith produces perseverance. Let perseverance finish its work so that you may be mature and complete, not lacking anything." Jarvis became clear about his spiritual goals and began building habits that allowed him to be more aligned and deepen his faith and connection with God.

Reflection

Pause—What's important to you in this season of your life? Not last year or five years from now. What is your purpose—what do you do that gives your life the most meaning right now? What are your values? What is your energy capacity? Do your daily choices reflect what matters most? Where have you drifted away from these anchor points?

Reflect—Create a *One-Page Miracle* for yourself. What do you want each of these areas to look like?

- The Biological Circle
- The Psychological Circle
- The Social Circle
- The Spiritual Circle

Regroup—Based on your answers above, what do you need to change to meet the filter: *Do my current actions and decisions get me what I want?* What do you need to change to bring all four areas into alignment: Biological, Psychological, Social, and Spiritual?

Chapter Eleven

Update Your Thinking

Renew Your Mind—
Not every thought deserves a seat at the table.[IP]

—Barbara Gustavson

OUR BRAINS PRODUCE tens of thousands of thoughts every single day. Some are helpful, some neutral, and some harmful. If you've ever noticed the same critical voice popping up again and again, you've experienced what psychologists call cognitive distortions—patterns of faulty thinking that warp reality.[34] [35] [36]

Dr. Amen calls these distortions ANTs, or Automatic Negative Thoughts.[37] They're the mental intruders that creep in without invitation and whisper things like, "You're not good enough," "This will never work," or "I should be stronger."

> Just because a thought shows up doesn't mean it deserves your agreement.

The problem with ANTs is that they sound convincing in the moment. They disguise themselves as truth when, in reality, they are nothing more than mental noise triggered by stress, fatigue, or old memories. Just because a thought shows up doesn't mean it deserves your agreement.

There are seven different types of ANTs that keep us from reaching our full potential.

- **All-or-Nothing ANT** features rigid, black-and-white thinking and sees no middle ground.

- **Always Negative ANT,** also known as Disqualifying the Positive, ignores any good evidence and focuses only on the bad and what's going wrong.

- **Fortune-Telling ANT** or Catastrophizing predicts the worst in every situation.

- **Mind-Reading ANT** assumes you know what others are thinking and that all thoughts are bad. Psychologists also call it Jumping to Conclusions.

- **Guilt-Beating ANT** is characterized by guilt and shame. It focuses on what you think you should do and is also called Should Statements.

- **Labeling ANT** forces you to reduce yourself or others to a single negative word.

- **Blaming ANT** or Personalization takes and gives excessive responsibility to yourself, others, or circumstances.

Question Your Thoughts

Emotional intelligence gives us the ability to recognize our thoughts and emotions and notice how they shape our thinking and behavior. Emotional agility takes it further. It allows us to move through emotions with curiosity instead of getting stuck in them.

Pixar's *Inside Out* paints an apt picture. Each character—Joy, Sadness, Anger, Fear, and Disgust—sits at the control panel of a young girl's mind. The story reminds us that every emotion has value. Even Sadness, which seems like a burden, is essential for healing and connection. The trouble comes when one emotion, or ANT, hijacks the control panel.

Our brains are wired with what psychologists call a **negativity bias**. Thousands of years ago, this mindset kept our ancestors alive. Every rustling bush put them on high alert—better to assume a predator than miss a real danger. Today, our brains still scan for danger, even when there's no real threat. That's why ANTs feel so believable. They fit the brain's built-in bias.

The good news is that neuroplasticity means the brain can be retrained. We can intentionally strengthen a **positivity bias** by also noticing what's good, what's true, and what's possible. We don't irresponsibly ignore problems; we balance the picture.

> Be transformed by the renewing of your mind.

Don't Fight What's Wrong. Train What's Right.

Though science didn't start to understand it until the eighteenth century, the apostle Paul recognized the brain's ability to reset as early as the first century. He told the people in Corinth, "Be transformed by the renewing of your mind." (1 Corinthians 12:2)

The transformation takes time and work, but many methods have been developed in the last fifty years to help with the process.

One powerful tool we can borrow from psychology to update our thinking is **cognitive reframing.** It invites us to step back and ask, "Is this thought accurate? Is it helpful? Is there another way to see this?" Regardless of which ANT shows up, you can restate the thought or question in a way that retrains your brain.

"I'll never get through this" becomes "This feels uncomfortable, I must be growing."

"She didn't reply, so she must be mad" becomes "She must be busy."

Every time you choose a healthier thought, you challenge your brain's negativity bias and rewire it.

Research by psychologist Barbara Fredrickson shows that having more positive emotions broadens our perspective and builds resilience. While giving yourself permission to acknowledge and feel negative emotions is necessary for releasing them, focusing only on what's wrong reinforces narrow, fear-driven pathways. Intentionally looking for what's going well trains our brain to see opportunities, strengths, and hope.[38]

Years ago, I attended a conference in Beaver Creek, Colorado, to face my fear of public speaking. We were given opportunities to share our story in front of a group of judges for feedback. I participated but found myself spiraling with my nervous system in full flight. I ended the day curled up in my hotel room after having a panic attack.

When I finally mustered the courage to return to the event, Michael Hyatt, the keynote speaker, was sharing how speaking drained him because he was an introvert. He also told us about the "secret toolkit" he used to prepare himself for speaking at events. One of his tools is a simple, silent prayer he offers when he feels fear or doubt. I've carried that prayer with me ever since.

*I am not here by accident. I have something important to share.
Someone in this room needs what I have to say.*

This prayer doesn't completely erase my fear, but it gives me the courage to take the next step. That's the power of catching a negative thought and reframing it into something that moves you forward.

Peggy Sue's Story

Peggie Sue Valentine—true to her name—had the biggest heart. She wasn't just my mom; she was one of my best friends and the one person who "got" me. She had a gift for seeing past the surface and understanding me in a way that few ever could.

In her fifties, she became a nurse and worked as a part-time LPN (Licensed Practical Nurse). I suspect she did that intentionally because it allowed her to keep caring for my dad, whose health was declining. She poured herself into others, both at work and at home, with a quiet strength that came at a cost.

Looking back, I can see how much she carried, often in silence. She didn't want her daughters to know the full weight of what was happening with my dad's health. We sensed it. We knew the stress was mounting, but she never said it out loud.

I'll always remember the moment my dad called with the news that my mom had suffered a stroke. It happened right after she received the news that her sister had passed away. I immediately rushed one hour away to the hospital, where they medevaced her. My mom could still talk when we got there, but within hours, her speech was gone, and she was incapacitated. After a month in the ICU, she moved to rehab. But only a few months later, just after she was discharged to go home, she suffered a brain bleed and never woke up.

Losing her this way was devastating. It was sudden and traumatic, leaving an ache that lingers today. But it also opened my eyes to something I now carry into my work: the hidden load of caregiving and the unspoken stress that impacts the brain and the body more than most understand. My mom was the picture of resilience, but she gave so much to everyone else that her own reserves ran dry.

> Harmful stress isn't just an emotional burden.

Mom's story reminds me why regrouping matters for leaders, caregivers, helpers, and anyone who is quietly carrying more than others realize. Harmful stress isn't just an emotional burden. It shows up in our health, in our nervous system, and in every organ, including our brain.

My mom's life continues to teach me. She taught me love, compassion, resilience, and the importance of caring for others. But she also taught me, without meaning to, the danger of carrying too much without Regrouping. When I help others today, I often think of her. Peggie Sue's story lives on as a reminder that the strongest hearts still need rest, care, and moments of peace.

Reflection

This reflection is one you'll want to return to often. By repeating these steps on a regular basis, you'll be able to Update Your Thinking.

Pause—Begin by catching your ANTs when they show up and questioning them. Katie Byron, author of the book *Loving What Is,* shares four questions to help shift negative thoughts. When you think, "I'm not strong enough," ask:

- "Is this true?"
- "Is this 100 percent true?"
- How do I feel or behave when I think "I'm not strong enough?"
- How do I feel when I don't think "I'm not strong enough?" [39]

Reflect—How would that statement change your thinking if you reframed it? Replace it with something more accurate and empowering. The truth of "I'm not good enough" might be "I don't have all the answers, but I have enough to move forward."

Regroup—REGROUP occurs when you repeat the process every time an ANT attempts to derail you. To Update Your Thinking even faster, grab a notebook and each night write three things that went well that day and three things you are grateful for. These don't have to be big to be effective. A kind word, a moment of laughter, or a small accomplishment will train your brain to look for the blessings in life. Over time, you will strengthen your positivity bias.

Chapter Twelve

Prioritize Brain Health

Taking time for you IS taking care of others.[IP]

—Barbara Gustavson

KARA AND I met over Zoom. Her mom and I had been college roommates more than thirty years before, and Kara was struggling in nursing school after being hospitalized because of a head injury.

She had been sitting on a friend's horse while looking at her phone when the horse suddenly bucked her off and kicked her in the head. After two weeks in the ICU and three months of recovery, she still had no memory of the accident.

Back at school, she could hear the teacher talking, but nothing registered. "When I try to do homework," she shared, "I just stare into space. I don't feel like hanging out with friends, and I can't stop crying. I just don't feel like myself anymore."

I shared resources for her to look into to support her brain's healing, and over the next few months, Kara took ownership of her healing. She found doctors who took her symptoms seriously and helped her implement practical brain health habits. Over time, she grew stronger, and so did her sense of self. She began to reclaim her life.

Mental Health Is Brain Health

After everything I've said about shifting your thinking and regulating your nervous system, you may expect me to focus more on mental health than brain health. However, many who emphasize only mental health overlook the very organ that drives the mind. Your brain is the command center behind your mental health, as well as your decisions, thoughts, emotions, relationships, and your capacity to take care of yourself.

Kara's story is living proof of the power of focusing on your brain health. We had a follow-up Zoom call after she started implementing treatments her doctor recommended, along with strategies I shared. She started to enjoy photography again and reconnected with her friends. Journaling about her trauma helped her confidence and happiness grow, and she'd begun to see herself in a new light. Kara realized she wasn't broken; she was healing.

Her story stirred something deep in me. I'd walked a similar path decades earlier—except my outcome was different.

The summer after my freshman year of college, I had a horse accident of my own. The horse I was riding reared, and as much as I tried to hold on, I flipped off and landed hard, hitting my head and breaking my back. They treated my back, but because I never lost consciousness, they overlooked the head injury.

When I returned to school, I noticed changes. Like Kara, I couldn't concentrate, and homework was impossible. I withdrew from my friends and spent nights crying alone. No one told me there were options that could help me recover, so I dropped out.

For three decades, I lived with the hidden cost of that brain injury. Doctors couldn't explain the ringing in my ears, brain fog, anxiety, depression, panic attacks, poor memory, and dizziness.

Then one day, during my late forties, I came across the book I mentioned earlier—the one that changed everything for me. It was the first time I understood that what I'd been facing wasn't just about mindset or emotions; it was about my brain. That single insight reframed everything.

In 2017, I finally decided to have a SPECT (Single Photon Emission Computed Tomography) scan of my brain. The results confirmed what I had suspected: I had several injuries, compounded by anxiety, stress, and trauma. But for the first time, the physicians gave me a clear plan forward. Through brain rehabilitation—including EMDR (Eye Movement Desensitization and Reprocessing), chiropractic adjustments, and neurofeedback—I experienced a real turnaround. It wasn't instant, but it was life-changing.

Telling the World

I'm sharing this because it matters. I've lived on both sides of the brain health journey—watching Kara's story of early intervention and proactive brain health, and walking my own long road of delayed help and silent struggle. Both stories reveal the same truth: when we care for the brain, we open the door to hope, healing, and resilience.

Dr. Amen often says, "Mental health is really brain health. When the brain works right, you work right; when the brain is troubled, you're much more likely to be troubled." This truth changed every realm of my life to such a degree that I now work for Dr. Amen and collaborate with clinicians and educators globally who use his methods and content in their practices.

As I've shared throughout these pages, mental health struggles aren't character flaws. They are signs that your brain needs support. When we begin to see these struggles as an organ problem rather than a character or moral problem, it shifts our outlook from helpless to hopeful, and we start focusing on the solution instead of only the symptom.

Look at the differences in perspectives when we shift our thinking from mental health to brain health.

Rethinking Mental Health Chart [IP]

MENTAL HEALTH	vs	BRAIN HEALTH
Reactive		Proactive
Crisis Focused		Solution Focused
Feels Heavy		Brings Relief
Produces Shame		Cultivates Compassion
Self-Diminishing		Self-Empowering
Draining		Energizing
Confusing		Clarifying
Creates Stigma		Sparks Curiosity

Kara had become a best-case scenario. She graduated on time with her class, became a critical care nurse, and now helps others with compassion rooted in her own experience. She's living proof that brain health tools can restore clarity, function, and hope.

I know the long road of silent suffering without recognizing the importance of brain health, and I know the freedom of finally discovering the tools to heal. That's why prioritizing brain health isn't optional. It's essential.

Katie's Story

In 2020, Katie, a natural health practitioner in New Zealand, endured one of the hardest seasons of her life. Everything seemed to collapse at once. She experienced a mild traumatic brain injury, and around the same time, she and her husband lost nearly 90 percent of their tourism business because of COVID-19. With two young children at home, she tried to keep pushing through. But beneath the surface, she was unraveling.

What makes Katie's story so powerful is that no one could see what she carried. From the outside, she functioned fine. Inside, she fought anxiety, rage, and depression every single day and felt guilty for not being the mom she wanted to be. Even her husband didn't fully know how bad things had gotten, so the severity of her pain remained hidden.

Katie tried everything—exercise, supplements, healthy eating. She followed all the advice, but nothing worked. The specialists kept giving her more tools, which only left her feeling more overwhelmed and more like a failure. The headaches, sleepless nights, and intense mood swings nearly tore her marriage apart.

Her breaking point came after a second suicide attempt. That rock-bottom moment changed everything. She began a year-long rehabilitation program, and during that time, a psychologist finally said the words that lifted a crushing weight off her shoulders: "It's not you, it's your brain."

Those words gave her permission to stop blaming herself and start healing. She took ownership of her recovery, choosing what mattered most, giving herself grace, and allowing both God and others to support her.

Katie often says a brain injury is invisible. And she's right. No one could see her battle. But what I admire most is how she's rebuilt her life with quiet strength. She no longer lets anyone else define her well-being. She lives with gratitude, focuses on meaningful relationships, and regularly checks where her energy goes. Her injury gave her a deeper empathy for others—an empathy that now radiates through everything she does.

Today, Katie often encourages others who feel stretched thin or exhausted. She reminds them that a bad day doesn't define their life. Hope can meet you in the smallest moments. One of the practical tools she shares is her "reset toolbox"—a low-bar routine that helps ground her, even on the hardest days. For her, that looks like a short yoga session, a daily walk, and starting the day with protein. These simple steps aren't about perfection; they're about persistence and grace.

Kara's and Katie's stories highlight what so many live with silently—the hidden pain of brain struggles. Their journeys remind us that prioritizing brain health is not about perfection, but about grace, persistence, and small daily practices that make healing possible.

That's why it's so important to understand your own brain—how it's wired, where it may struggle, and how to care for it in practical ways.

Twelve Foundational Principles of Brain Health

Again, much of the following content is adapted and shared with permission from Dr. Amen and Amen Clinics. His decades of research and clinical work have contributed significantly to how we understand, support, and protect brain health.

Humans have adopted skincare regimens, exercise habits, diet techniques, and other health routines, but we don't encourage brain health regimens, even though our brain drives everything else.

These twelve foundational principles highlight what the brain needs to stay healthy, as well as the factors that can put it at risk.[40] They seem simple at first glance, but don't underestimate them. When you truly understand and apply these principles, they can create a foundation for wellness that supports how you think, lead, and live.

> Humans have adopted all kinds of health routines, but don't encourage brain health regimens, even though our brain drives everything else.

Principle #1. Your Brain Is Involved in Everything You Do

The moment-by-moment functioning of your brain controls the way you think, feel, act, and how well you get along with others. It is involved in your daily decisions, including when you take on too many responsibilities or feel isolated and overwhelmed.

Principle #2. When Your Brain Works Right, You Work Right. When Your Brain Is Troubled, You Have Trouble in Your Life.

When the brain functions well, it supports clear thinking, stable moods, good decision-making, and overall resilience. People with healthy brain activity often experience greater focus, energy, and emotional balance.

However, when the brain is troubled—whether from injury, poor lifestyle habits, or other risk factors—life often becomes more difficult. Struggles with mood, focus, relationships, or health may reflect what's happening in the brain rather than a personal weakness.

Research in brain health over the past several decades has emphasized that many challenges traditionally labeled as "mental illness" are often better understood as brain health issues—conditions that can improve when we care for the brain itself.

Principle #3. Your Brain is the Most Complicated Organ in the Universe

Your brain contains about 100 billion cells and more connections than all the stars in the universe. Scientists estimate its storage capacity at three million hours of TV shows. At approximately three pounds, it makes up only about 2 percent of your body weight, but it consumes 20–30 percent of your calories, 20 percent of your oxygen and blood flow, and almost 80 percent of the water you drink. This means our food intake and hydration truly matter, and anything that damages our heart or blood vessels can ultimately damage the brain.

Principle #4. Your Brain is Soft—and It's Housed in a Very Hard Skull

Your brain has the same consistency as egg whites or gelatin. Sharp ridges inside the skull make it vulnerable during jarring motions or head injuries. Even mild traumatic brain injuries (TBIs) can negatively impact lives, but because psychiatrists rarely look at the brain, most don't know about the damage. Undiagnosed brain injuries are a major cause of suicide, homicide, depression, ADHD, learning problems, domestic violence, and incarceration. Kara's story, my own experience, and Katie's journey all intersect in this fact. We are reminders that head trauma can change everything, but healing is still possible. Sadly, about two million TBIs occur each year. Protecting your brain must be a priority.

Principle # 5. Your Brain Has Needs that Must Be Met

In order for the brain to function properly and work at optimal efficiency, it needs:

- ❖ Healthy blood flow (to deliver oxygen, vitamins, and essential minerals to the brain)
- ❖ Proper hydration
- ❖ Physical and mental exercise
- ❖ Stimulation (new learning)
- ❖ Fuel (healthy food)
- ❖ Hormones
- ❖ A strong immune system
- ❖ An efficient waste management system to detoxify your body
- ❖ Adequate sleep
- ❖ Meaning and purpose in your life
- ❖ More than ever, we need to be socially connected

Principle #6. Many Things Hurt the Brain and Should Be Avoided

Brain imaging research over several decades has identified key risk factors that can harm the brain and impact how we think, feel, and function. Dr. Amen developed the acronym **BRIGHT MINDS** as a practical way to remember these major risk areas:

- ❖ Blood flow
- ❖ Retirement/Aging
- ❖ Inflammation
- ❖ Genetics
- ❖ Head trauma

❖ Toxins

❖ Mental health issues

❖ Immunity/Infections

❖ Neurohormones

❖ Diabetes/Obesity

❖ Sleep Apnea

Principle #7. Many Things Help the Brain

Fortunately, there are effective strategies to minimize risk and boost brain function—many of which align with the BRIGHT MINDS framework. One of Dr. Amen's core teachings is to regularly ask yourself, "Is this good or bad for my brain?" This simple question can help guide daily choices and build long-term habits that support brain health.

> Regularly ask yourself,
> "Is this good or bad for my brain?"

Principle #8. Certain brain systems tend to do specific things.

Like an orchestra, all parts of your brain need to be working together to make you the best you can be.

The Prefrontal Cortex is the "Boss" of the Brain. This brain system helps you focus, plan, make decisions, follow through, and control impulses. It's like the CEO of your brain. When it struggles, you'll have trouble focusing, you'll procrastinate, experience poor follow-through, impulsivity, disorganization, and act without thinking. Sometimes a struggle in the prefrontal cortex is linked to ADHD, lack of motivation, or poor judgment. You can take care of this brain system by getting enough sleep, avoiding alcohol and marijuana (which can lower blood flow), using goal-setting exercises, breaking big projects into smaller steps, and eating protein-rich foods for steady energy. Supplements like omega-3s can also boost prefrontal activity.

The Anterior Cingulate Gyrus is the Brain's Gear Shift. This helps you switch attention, adapt to change, and go with the flow. When it struggles, you may get stuck on worries, hold grudges, have repetitive thoughts, or wrestle with flexibility. It emerges as anxiety, obsessive thinking, or rigid behavior. You can support this brain system by practicing flexibility—shift your routines, try new things, and practice letting go. Supplements like saffron, as well as calming practices like meditation and journaling, may also help calm this area.

The Deep Limbic System Is Your Mood Regulator. It sets your emotional tone, gives you perspective, and helps you connect with meaning. When the deep limbic system struggles, you feel sadness, have low energy, experience negative thinking and mood swings, and become vulnerable to depression. People may feel more disconnected or hopeless when this system becomes overactive. You can help your this brain system by building daily gratitude practices, spending time with uplifting people, exercising (especially outdoors), practicing forgiveness, and leaning on faith or purpose. Nutrients like omega-3s, vitamin D, or SAMe (S-Adenosylmethionine) may also help.

The Basal Ganglia Is the Brain's "Anxiety Center". The Basal Ganglia helps control movement, but also plays a key role in motivation, drive, and setting the body's anxiety level. When it struggles, you will worry excessively and feel tension, fear, shyness, panic attacks, or perfectionism. Too little activity here can also cause low motivation and a lack of follow-through.

Physical exercise, calming breathing practices, and relaxation techniques like yoga will help keep your basal ganglia healthy. Supplements such as magnesium, theanine, or GABA support may promote focus.

Principle #9. Understanding Your Brain Helps You Know How to Support It.

These basic descriptions can give you insight into your own mind. For example, if you discover you have low frontal lobe activity or your Basal Ganglia struggles, you need clear goals to support your brain. Write these goals and ask, "Does my behavior fit what I want?"

Principle #10. Psychiatric "Illnesses" Are Not Single or Simple Disorders; Each of the Multiple Types Requires Its Own Treatment

A one-size-fits-all approach to mental health often leads to potential misdiagnosis, repeated setbacks, and deep frustration. Over time, brain imaging research has shown that many conditions commonly labeled under a single diagnosis actually present in multiple patterns. For example, research has identified seven types of anxiety and depression and an equal number of kinds of ADD. Addiction boasts six different types and overeating has five.

If you or someone you know struggles with any of these, awareness of your brain type and working closely with a qualified physician or specialist can help you gain clarity on treatment.

Principle #11. Your Brain Only Has So Much Reserve

Brain reserve is the extra cushion of brain function that helps you handle stress. Like a healthy immune system helps you when you're exposed to the most violent strains of virus, a brain that has its needs met can get you through some of the most difficult times.

Principle #12. Looking at the Brain Changes Everything

Brain imaging has proven that we are not stuck with the brain we have. This is perhaps the most exciting and hopeful lesson of all. We can make our brains better by taking tiny steps to improve how they function. With a better brain comes a better life and better mental health. Your brain can start improving tomorrow if you start making intentional choices today. Dr. Amen recommends the following:

1. Fall in love with your brain and develop "brain envy."
2. Avoid things that hurt your brain.
3. Do things that help your brain.[41]

Brain Types

When I was a child, I found it amazing that no two people share the same fingerprint. It made me wonder how something so small could hold something so personal. Years later, I discovered something even more mind-blowing. Of all the brain scans studied to date, they've never found two brains exactly alike.

Every brain tells its own story. And yet, beneath that uniqueness, our brains share patterns that explain why certain challenges and struggles show up the way they do. Understanding these patterns can offer us clarity about things that used to be confusing. We can recognize the parts of our lives that energize us and those that quietly drain us. This knowledge can also help us learn how to support our brains so we work with the patterns instead of against them.

No two recoveries look the same; however, research shows that certain brain activity patterns—what they call *brain types*—reveal both our strengths and our vulnerabilities. These patterns simply reveal why your brain might react with worry, get stuck in overwhelm, or feel weighed down by mood. And just as importantly, they point to practical ways to restore balance and energy.

It turns out that there are five primary brain types based on SPECT imaging and decades of clinical research. Each type reflects different activity patterns that influence mood, focus, energy, and behavior, and they combine to form eleven more complex patterns. Each type also has its own strengths. Here's a simple overview:

Brain Type 1: Balanced

This is the most sought-after pattern. Brain activity and blood flow are generally even and well-regulated, leading to stable moods, good focus, and healthy energy.

Brain Type 2: Spontaneous

A Spontaneous brain type can be linked to overactivity in the cerebellum and underactivity in the prefrontal cortex. People with a Spontaneous brain pattern may be more creative, adventurous, and full of ideas, but can also be impulsive, easily distracted, or restless.

Brain Type 3: Persistent

Characterized by increased activity in the anterior cingulate gyrus. People tend to be more goal-driven, detail-oriented, and focused, but may struggle with being flexible, getting stuck on worries, or having trouble shifting gears.

Brain Type 4: Sensitive

Tied to heightened activity in the limbic system. Individuals with this brain type are empathetic, deep-feeling, and intuitive, but may also be vulnerable to mood swings, sadness, or low energy.

Brain Type 5: Cautious

A Cautious brain is related to increased activity in the basal ganglia. People often are especially careful, thoughtful, and prepared, but may also lean toward anxiety, tension, or excessive worry.

For those who are natural givers and supporters, understanding these brain types is especially important. Again, each type carries its own resilience and strengths, but also its own vulnerabilities that may quietly lead to burnout when caregiving or leading others.

For instance, the balanced type may take on too much without pausing; the spontaneous type may overcommit; the persistent type may struggle to let go; the sensitive type may absorb others' pain; and the cautious type may wear down under constant worry.

Recognizing these patterns helps caregivers not only extend compassion to others but also to themselves, so they can set healthy boundaries, protect their energy, and continue showing up with strength and clarity.

Reflection

Pause—Pausing isn't just a nice idea; it's essential for brain health. If we pay attention to our ultradian rhythm—that 90 to 120-minute brain cycle we discussed earlier—we can build intentional pauses into our day and work *with* our brain instead of against it.

Reflect—How do the brain types and principles mentioned help you better understand the way your brain operates?

Regroup—What's one small daily step you can take to support your brain? Start paying attention to your focus and energy levels throughout the day. Instead of pushing harder, you can pause and listen to what your body and brain need. It might be as simple as drinking a glass of water at the top of every hour.

Additionally, take the free assessment at brainhealthassessment.com to learn your own brain type and discover practical ways to support it.

Now that you've learned the steps for REGROUP, you can see that it is possible to lead, serve, and live without running on fumes. REGROUP isn't about checking out and abandoning responsibility. It's the intentional breath before reacting, a designed pause that helps you reset, refocus, and reach your goals.

This isn't about changing who you are; it's about learning to support your flame so it keeps burning strong.

PART 3

REBUILD

Chapter Thirteen

Your Circle of Support

If you want to go fast, go alone.
If you want to go far, go together.

—African Proverb

OUR INVISIBLE LOADS will often be the heaviest weight we carry. Responsibilities, emotional labor, and quiet caregiving create pressure to always hold it together. The tasks seldom come with recognition, and they drain enormous amounts of energy.

For years, I carried my emotional caregiving role in silence. From the outside, I looked fine. Inside, I was falling apart. Things began to change only after I admitted I couldn't do it alone.

We often talk about leaders and caregivers as anchors for others. But even anchors need something solid to hold onto.[IP] Resilience doesn't grow in isolation; it requires connection.

My friend, Sheri, experienced this in an unexpected way. She was part of a group of business owners led by a mentor named Chris Oakley. When Chris tragically passed away at the young age of thirty-six, the group faced a choice: either disband or keep going. They chose to honor Chris' legacy by strengthening their bonds and moving forward as

Community on Demand, a group that still meets regularly and operates a nonprofit arm to provide scholarships for high school seniors and funding for disaster relief efforts.

> Boundaries protect your energy; support restores it.

Their story is a reminder that resilience is relational. Support teams matter. They prove boundaries and connections should coexist. Boundaries protect your energy; support restores it. Together, they help you REGROUP and operate from a place of strength.

Create a Circle of Support

Strong social ties are some of the greatest predictors of resilience. The CDC has highlighted that caregivers without support are far more likely to experience depression and health problems.

A therapist once told me, "Never worry alone." This is where your support team comes in. It doesn't have to be a large group. It might be a friend who listens without judging or fixing, a counselor who helps you process, or a mentor who reminds you of your strengths when you forget them.

When I cared for my dad, my mom's best friend, Gail, a retired nurse, became one of the most important voices in my circle. She helped me make difficult medical decisions on his behalf, decisions that broke my heart but that had to be made. Gail never judged me when guilt crept in. She was a sounding board and a safe place to be honest.

Even after the chapter of caring for my dad closed, I continue to have a strong support circle. Various friends, my husband, and a coach. I also have a strong, small circle of local friends. Each year, we have a getaway at the Outer Banks. These times that have become anchors I fiercely protect.

My friends also lighten things up when I give in to my tendency to be too serious. They offer a welcome distraction during those times I needed a break from the weight of caring. I am grateful for the many wonderful people in my life. Still, I keep my inner circle intentionally small. I know who fills me up, and I deliberately choose who I spend time with.

Creating a circle of strength doesn't mean cutting people out. It means being clear about what you need to stay whole. Boundaries are not intended to be walls; they're acts of care that protect your energy and your ability to keep showing up aligned with your purpose.

Your circle may include professionals. Depending on the season or situation, I've sought mentors to guide me, each offering wisdom in their own way. I've also leaned on my therapist to carry things I couldn't place on friends or family.

> Boundaries are acts of care that protect your energy and your ability to keep showing up.

Reflection

Pause—Take a moment to consider who you currently have in your circle. Is it a circle of strength? When we return to the principle of Guarding Your Margins, we realize we might need to re-evaluate our inner circle.

Reflect—Write down the name of at least one person who is or should be in your circle of strength. Think of those who listen without judgment, remind you of your values, or give you space to breathe when life feels heavy. This could be a friend, mentor, faith leader, or professional who can support you.

Regroup—Reach out to the person whose name you wrote down. Let them know you need someone to help you stay strong. This may make you feel vulnerable, but vulnerability is often the doorway to strength.

My own circle of strength has included Gail, my therapist, trusted friends, yearly retreats, and wise mentors. It's not flashy, but it's real. And it's what allows me to keep operating from alignment, even in seasons when everything feels overwhelming.

Remember, resilience doesn't live in isolation. It grows in connection. What you carry matters, even if no one sees it. And you don't have to carry it alone.

Chapter Fourteen

Redefining Balance

*Balance is not about juggling everything at once,
but knowing when to give each aspect of life its due
attention.*

—Aloo Denish Obiero

FIND WORK-LIFE BALANCE. Hustle harder. Slow down and rest, but make sure you're endlessly productive. But that kind of balance—the perfect, everything-in-its-place kind—doesn't exist. And when we treat balance like an all-or-nothing achievement, it leaves many of us feeling like we've failed before we even begin.

No wonder so many feel as if we're falling short. We like the idea of balance, but for most people—especially in seasons of caregiving, loss, or rebuilding—it becomes another impossible standard.

Balance is often defined as keeping all areas of life in perfect proportion. But real life doesn't work like that. When someone you love starts to decline, their body needs time to heal, or your capacity is limited, you can't always give equal energy to work, relationships, rest, and protecting your flame.

I'm not the first person to realize that slowing down your pace isn't weakness. It's wisdom in motion.[IP]

A Better Way to Think About Balance

When it comes to wellness, people often talk about "balance" as if it means giving equal energy to every area of life. But that kind of balance is rigid and unrealistic. Life rarely stays evenly distributed—especially when you're carrying more than usual, supporting loved ones, healing, or navigating change.

> When balance stops being an all-or-nothing expectation, it becomes something we can actually work with.

True balance isn't about perfection. It's about movement. It's about finding better balance in a season, not perfect balance for a lifetime. It's not about giving equal time to everything. It's about recognizing which areas of life hold the most weight in the moment.

Some days that means shifting a little more energy toward rest, other days it's showing up fully in one area while letting something else be "good enough." When balance stops being an all-or-nothing expectation, it becomes something we can actually work with, and it gives you permission to REGROUP.

Equilibrium offers a more realistic way of thinking and living. With our physical body, equilibrium isn't about staying perfectly still—our body constantly adjusts to stay within a healthy range. Our bodies naturally shift, respond, and recalibrate throughout the day to keep us healthy. Life works the same way. We don't need to live perfectly balanced lives; we need the capacity to notice when we're out of range and gently adjust.

Better balance honors those small recalibrations—choosing alignment over perfection, harmony over control, and steadying yourself rather than trying to hold everything up at once. We don't have to wait until a crisis to adjust; in fact, the more we adjust now, the more resilient we are.

It's not about keeping everything equal—it's about staying steady as things shift and when life gets chaotic, adjust as necessary. Andrea Edmondson says, "You don't have to break to break through." Equilibrium allows your priorities to flex without losing your center.

Regroup Restores Your Equilibrium

This is where REGROUP comes in. It's the intentional pause that lets you realign, refocus, and redirect your energy toward what matters most in the season you're in. Instead of chasing perfect balance, you learn to anchor yourself. That steadiness is what protects your wellness and keeps your flame from burning out.

Equilibrium keeps your body centered through constant change. Not every part gets the same weight; yet they exist in perfect harmony. Equilibrium means your system remains stable because it listens and adjusts.

When blood sugar drops, you feel hunger. When your heart rate climbs, your body tells you to slow down. When your nervous system is overwhelmed, it tries to ground you.

You feel it when something in your body is off. But if we listen, we discover the same thing happens emotionally, socially, and spiritually. Every part of our being attempts to keep us in equilibrium. Regrouping helps you hear those signals instead of overriding them.

This shift from *balance* to *equilibrium* gives you freedom.

- Freedom to focus on what matters without guilt.
- Freedom to honor your limits without labeling them as weakness.
- Freedom to let go of the myth that everything has to run at 100% all the time.

Whether you call it balance, equilibrium, homeostasis, or harmony, what matters is the meaning you give it. Balance or equilibrium isn't something we achieve and keep; it's something we practice and return to. There will always be seasons where one area of life takes more space than another. That doesn't mean you've failed—it means you're human. The goal is to keep finding your way back to what matters, making micro-adjustments along the way.

> Equilibrium isn't something we achieve and keep; it's something we practice and return to.

How the REGROUP Framework Supports Equilibrium

Each element of the REGROUP framework creates the conditions for internal and external equilibrium.

R **Resilience** allows us to bend without breaking. Remembering our strength gives us permission to let our priorities shift while staying grounded in our values.

E **Energy** awareness reminds us that our energy is limited and reminds us to optimize and monitor our reserves to give our bodies and brain everything they need.

G **Guarding your margin** keeps you steady and clear because you fiercely protect your boundaries. White space isn't laziness; it's breathing room.

R **Regulating the nervous system** creates productive peace. It prevents spiraling into panic or over-functioning when things get out of sync.

O **Operating from alignment** tells the world what you value. You evaluate whether your choices reflect your real priorities, not just outside pressure.

U **Updated thinking** clears outdated beliefs like "I should be able to do it all" and replaces them with more stabilized and accurate reasoning.

P **Prioritizing brain health** allows for better decision-making, rest, and self-awareness—core ingredients for any sustainable equilibrium.

You don't have to do everything equally. You don't have to keep it all perfectly together.

You do need to know how to REGROUP.
Reflection

Pause—Pausing is always the first step in REGROUP: stop, breathe, evaluate your actions. Does what you're experiencing fit any of the letters of the REGROUP Framework?

Reflect—Instead of asking, "Do I have balance?" ask yourself these questions:

- What would bring me a little *more balance* right now?
- What is currently out of balance in my life?
- Where can I let go of trying to have perfect balance?

That small shift in language changes the pressure we put on ourselves. It creates space for grace and progress rather than perfection.

Regroup—Equilibrium allows us to live in *graceful imbalance*—a state of rhythm and responsiveness, not rigidity. It's not about staying centered all the time. It's about knowing how to *return* to center when things drift. Which area of REGROUP would you like to begin working on?

Chapter Fifteen

The Art of Savoring

To live is the rarest thing in the world.
Most people exist, that is all.

—Oscar Wilde

DO YOU REMEMBER the old Big Red gum commercials? Two people kissing at a train station, friends laughing together, parents holding kids close—the world seemed to slow for just a few seconds while the unforgettable jingle played:

"Kiss a little longer, Hold hands a little longer,

Hold tight a little longer, Say goodbye a little longer…"

Those commercials resonated because they captured something universal—a longing to stretch the best moments of life, to make them linger. We want to savor the beautiful memories.

An Antidote to Burnout

Chronic stress, burnout, and the weight of high expectations can throw us into survival mode. We begin to feel as though we exist without truly living. The REGROUP Framework offers practical tools to make us come alive again and savor the sweetness of the everyday.

We discover simple joy in a meaningful conversation, the sound of rain, and laughter that catches us off guard. These moments may be small, but they become powerful anchors when life feels heavy—those "Big Red" moments that make time slow down.

Neuroscience backs this kind of savoring. Research shows that finding joy in the everyday pleasures protects us from stress, increases gratitude, and deepens overall life satisfaction. When we savor, the brain releases its reward chemical—dopamine–strengthening memory circuits so that joy leaves a deeper imprint.[42]

Positive emotions expand our perspective and build lasting inner resources like creativity, resilience, and connection. When we savor, we aren't just enjoying the moment; we're wiring our brains to look for more of it. Taking time to savor is not indulgent; it's intelligent and a brain-healthy way to keep burnout at bay. It's how you reclaim the energy to live fully.

It's Okay to Take Off the Cape

For a long time, I believed it was my job to carry everything for my family, for clients, for everyone else. I was a classic enabler who would slip into the role of rescuer, convincing myself that if I just worked harder, sacrificed more, or "figured it out," I could save the day.

> It's okay to take off your cape once in a while.

Then one day, my friend Johnnie said something that stopped me in my tracks. She told me, "It's okay to take off your cape once in a while."

Those words landed with both relief and conviction. I realized I wore my "cape" constantly, showing up like the world's weight was mine alone to carry. But savoring—learning to linger in the goodness of life—gave me permission to take the cape off.

A coach once gave me a simple but profound exercise. She asked me to draw a line down the middle of a piece of paper. On the left, I listed all the ways I tried to save the world. On the right, I listed ways I can *savor* it instead.

The results shifted my lens. Instead of fixating on what needed rescuing, I began to live more in the present moment. I slowed down when eating instead of rushing through meals. I started honoring my morning and evening rhythms. I stopped automatically jumping in whenever I sensed someone needed help. I let others support my dad and focused on creating meaningful moments with him. One of his favorite things was watching the birds, and those quiet times became some of our most precious. Savoring doesn't erase hardship. It doesn't mean ignoring the challenges. It balances the weight. It lets the good and the hard sit in equilibrium, so life doesn't feel one-dimensional.

Reflection

Pause—Learning to savor requires awareness. Take a moment to consider where your cape might feel heavy from helping others, and imagine what it feels like to set it down.

Reflect—Take a piece of paper and draw a line down the middle. On the left, list all the ways you try to "save the world." On the right, record the ways you can savor the world more.

For example:

Left: "I step in and fix problems before anyone has a chance to help."

Right: "I take a breath, delegate what I can, instead of doing it all myself."

Left: "I rush through dinner so I can clean up and move on."

Right: "I slow down, and eat with gratitude for the food and the hands that made it possible."

Regroup—Choose one thing from your left column and intentionally practice the action you wrote on the right for at least one week. Continue to shift from your left list to the right list. One day, you'll look back and notice how much more you're savoring the moments that matter.

These small acts of savoring build even more resilience. They reawaken color in gray seasons. They remind you that you're not just here to carry the weight of the world—you're here to experience its wonder too. Savoring doesn't deny pain or hardship. But it does make space for the good to stand beside it. And sometimes, experiencing life a "little longer" is exactly what helps your flame shine bright.

Chapter Sixteen

Leading with Hope

Hope doesn't take no for an answer.

—Unknown

LEADERSHIP, CAREGIVING, AND showing up for others can feel heavy. We give and give because we care. Driven by compassion, we can slip into overgiving, overfunctioning, and overextending if we're not careful. The impact we make becomes compromised when it's built on depletion.

The REGROUP Framework allows us to shift from saving to savoring. That shift not only supports our resilience, it builds hope.

Hope is more than wishful thinking. The strength it carries helps us keep moving, even when circumstances or people say something is impossible. Hope believes something good can still happen, so it keeps looking for a way forward. Fear gives up at the first obstacle, but hope pushes back and says, *"Not yet isn't the same as never."*

Hope as a Neurostrategy

Psychologist Charles Snyder defined hope as a cognitive framework—a combination of agency (the belief that you can reach your goal) and pathways (the ability to identify multiple routes to get there).[43] Hope is brain-based motivation. It helps us act, adapt, and persist—even when Plan A fails.

For leaders, hope is essential. It fuels clarity during uncertainty, creates forward momentum when things feel stuck, and, like resilience, it's something you can build.

But hope needs connection. It doesn't grow in isolation. It grows in conversation. Sharing your challenges and goals with others lights up your brain with new possibilities. Dialogue sparks ideas, encouragement, and momentum.

> Hope needs connection. It doesn't grow in isolation.

Hope isn't meant to be carried alone. There are moments when a team, a family, or a group of friends needs to pause, reflect, and realign together. This kind of regrouping goes beyond individual reflection. It creates a shared space where people can be honest, listen deeply, and reset collectively.

When I lead retreats, that's exactly what we're doing. We carve out intentional space to step back from the noise, take a clear look at where we are, and reconnect with what matters most. It's powerful to watch a group not just talk, but truly regroup—clarifying direction, refreshing energy, and rebuilding trust. That kind of shared reset has a way of breathing life into people who may have lost sight of their "why."

This kind of regrouping isn't limited to teams. It can happen around a kitchen table, on a short drive, or during a quiet walk with someone you love. It's often the simplest conversations that become turning points. A few thoughtful questions, a willingness to listen, and a little time can help people breathe again and see possibilities they couldn't see before.

And this is where hope becomes leadership. Once you've experienced the power of regrouping for yourself, you can create that space for others. You become the one who gently invites people to slow down, reflect, and realign. It's a quiet, steady influence—the kind that can shift the emotional temperature of a room and remind people they're not alone.

Abraham Lincoln once said, "If I had six hours to chop down a tree, I'd spend the first four sharpening the ax." Regrouping is sharpening the ax. Hope gives it direction. When people have a clear sense of hope and the space to realign, they move forward with more strength, focus, and courage.

> REGROUP functions better in how you frame your situation.

Unintentionally, many leaders internally feel isolated and carry the weight of leadership alone. However, if you or someone you know is facing burnout, loss, or transition, feeling isolated can add to feelings of despair. A circle of support can help give you hope. But remember, REGROUP functions better in how you frame your situation and who you invite into that framing. Your words matter. Your support systems matter.

Hope and resilience are companions. Together, they form a foundation that allows you to lead boldly, live sustainably, and regroup whenever needed.

Reflection

Pause—Take a minute to consider how hopeful you feel. Where in your life do you feel the most alive, expectant, or steady? What people, places, or actions give you hope? Naming them strengthens your brain's ability to return to these anchors when things feel uncertain.

Reflect—If you've been feeling more tired than energized, discouraged than confident, or caught in cycles of worry, these may be quiet signals that your hope reserves are low. Hope isn't something you "should" just have; it's something that can be built and replenished. Noticing what drains your hope is just as important as identifying what fuels it. Taking care of yourself will help you build hope

Regroup—Revisit the Resilience part of the REGROUP Framework to remind yourself of the strength you've already demonstrated. Hope isn't about ignoring the hard things. It's about remembering your capacity to adapt, your support systems, and the moments that prove you can keep moving forward. It's realizing how strong you are. Choose one practical action—rest, connection, a walk, a meaningful conversation—and let that be your spark to rekindle hope.

Chapter Seventeen

Who Am I Becoming?

*Sometimes, who you become while chasing your goal
is better than actually hitting your goal.*

—Unknown

WHEN LOSS, STRESS, or unexpected change disrupts life,
it can leave us staring into the mirror, asking the haunting
question: *Who am I now?*

That question feels heavy, as if the ground beneath us has
shifted. But what if we changed the wording just slightly?
What if instead we asked: *Who am I becoming?*

That shift changes everything. It reminds us that our
Identity is not fixed; it's alive, evolving with every season.
REGROUP doesn't ask you to dismiss your past or minimize your present. It simply reminds you that your past
doesn't dictate your future.

What you've walked through—the heartbreaks, the
mistakes, the victories—are not wasted. It's been shaping
a deeper strength within you. My friend Patti is a powerful
example of what it looks like to embrace who you're becoming in the midst of deep loss.

Patti's Story

My dear friend, Patti Hanrath, thought caregiving would define her forever. She experienced some difficult days during her caregiving journey. Burnout had stripped her of energy, clarity, and joy, and she couldn't imagine ever feeling whole again.

Years before her husband, Joe, moved into long-term care, Patti lived in constant survival mode. Joe's Early Onset Alzheimer's filled her days and nights with uncertainty. She carried the quiet heartbreak of watching the man she loved struggle through sleepless nights and endless wandering as pieces of him slowly slipped away. The exhaustion of holding everything together was something words couldn't quite capture.

When Joe finally transitioned into long-term care, the silence of the house that first night crushed her. I'll always remember Patti telling me how she sat on the couch and sobbed, finally

> Moving forward doesn't mean you love any less.

confronting the reality that Joe would never come home again. In that deep grief, something unexpected surfaced—a flicker of hope. Knowing he was safe and cared for, Patti also realized she still had a life.

Moving forward didn't mean she loved Joe any less. In fact, it was the opposite. Loving him deeply also meant loving herself enough to keep living. That realization became a quiet turning point. Patti began to shift her view of caregiving. Instead of making it her identity, it became a chapter that shaped her and gave her a depth of growth and wisdom she hadn't recognized before.

Her reset didn't happen overnight. It started in small, intentional ways—allowing herself to rest without guilt, inviting joy back in through simple pleasures like reading, walking, and spending time with friends who reminded her she was more than "Joe's wife and caregiver." Her questions shifted from "Who am I without caregiving?" to "Who am I becoming because of this journey?"

That change in perspective helped her see growth where she once only saw loss. While caregiving shaped her deeply, it did not define her. What defined her was the woman who loved fiercely, endured the fire, and chose to keep living fully.

Even after Joe passed away, she carried his love with her. Moving on never meant leaving him behind—it meant honoring him by continuing to live. Joe had been her partner in life, and even as Alzheimer's changed everything, their love endured. That love gave her the courage to begin again.

Patti's reset was never about erasing loss; it was about transforming it into courage, love, and the strength to become more fully herself.

Start Fresh Without Starting from Scratch

I mentioned earlier that this book can be like a new beginning. When people think of a fresh start, they often imagine wiping the slate completely clean, as if nothing has happened. But you can't erase what's happened in the past. Instead, you begin from where you are.

> Big impact doesn't require big burnout.

A fresh start isn't always about starting over. It's starting forward. You carry your wisdom, love, and hard-earned lessons with you, even if current circumstances don't change. It's a time to remember big impact doesn't require big burnout.[IP]

I once worked with a client who believed they had nothing left to build on, that they had "ruined everything" because of a series of setbacks. But as we talked, it became clear their experience had developed tools and strengths. Every moment mattered. They didn't need a blank slate; they needed to reframe their story. They began to see that their past wasn't a liability; it was a library. Every chapter they had lived gave them resources for the road ahead.

Words, mistakes, and roles do not define you. Your identity is living and breathing, constantly reshaped by experience. When you see identity as a process rather than a destination, you release the pressure of having to "figure it all out." You start fresh, not from nothing, but from a place rich with what you've learned.

The Beauty of Brokenness

In the ancient Japanese practice of kintsugi, broken pottery finds new life with veins of gold. The cracks don't disappear. An artisan carefully fills and highlights them, turning what once seemed ruined into something exquisite. The scars don't weaken the vessel. They make it more precious. What was once a flaw becomes the most beautiful part of the piece.

Life works the same way. Chronic stress, caregiving, and crisis can leave us feeling cracked and broken. In those moments, it's easy to believe that being broken means being less. But hope and resilience are the gold. They don't erase what happened. They reshape us.

The strength of your story doesn't come from avoiding the breaking; it comes from the way the light shines through the places that have been repaired. What once felt like the end can become the most powerful, radiant part of your story.

When you allow those gold-filled cracks to be seen—first to yourself and then to others—you give permission for healing, not just for you, but for those watching your journey. What once felt like loss can become your greatest source of connection and strength, because your story now holds the gold of what you've learned.

Reflection

Pause—Take a moment and look for the gold veins that you thought meant you were broken, but now you realize make you beautiful.

Reflect—To step into who you are becoming, ask yourself:

- What part of my past strengthens me today?
- What am I ready to release so I can grow forward?
- What would it look like to begin again without starting over?

Regroup—Grab a piece of paper and write yourself a letter that begins with "This is who I am becoming . . ." It doesn't have to be perfect or polished. Let your pen and thoughts move freely. The words that surface often reveal strength and clarity you didn't realize you carried.

A season of giving of yourself is not the end of your story. It's the start of a new chapter. You can begin again, right where you are.

Your history is not your destiny.

Your past is not wasted.

Every step, every setback, every ache of your heart has prepared you for what's next. You didn't lose yourself in that season. You get to discover who you were always becoming.

That's the beauty of a life ready to REGROUP.

You can access exclusive REGROUP bonuses by submitting the order number from your book purchase receipt at discovernextstep.com/regroup-book.com.

APPENDIX

Appendix A:
Regrouping in Real Life^{IP}

Taking time to pause is one of the keys to the REGROUP Framework. Below you'll find some ideas to help you get started. Whether you only have sixty seconds between meetings, an afternoon to yourself, or a full season to step back, every moment will prove valuable.

You don't need to try everything on the list or look for the perfect potion. Simply choose the idea that feels most doable in the moment or let them spark a new idea that works better for you. Some practices may become part of your regular rhythm. Others you'll save for the days you need something different. However you use them, let these be your permission slips to breathe and reset.

Regrouping Ideas: Small (5 Minutes or Less)

Quick resets you can do anywhere to shift your energy, clear your mind, and reconnect with yourself.

- Step outside and take three slow, intentional breaths while focusing on a single sound in your environment.
- Write down one thing you're grateful for and one thing you're letting go of today.
- Drink a full glass of water, and notice the sensation.
- Stretch your shoulders, neck, and back, and name something you're grateful for.
- Close your eyes and picture a place where you've felt deeply safe and at peace.
- Sit, close your eyes, and listen to a calming or energizing song.
- Send a quick, encouraging message to someone who's been on your mind.
- Step away from your phone or computer and focus your eyes on a distant object for thirty seconds to reset visual and mental strain.
- Light a candle and pause to breathe in the scent.
- Hold a warm mug of tea or coffee in your hands and focus on its warmth.
- Stand barefoot on the floor or grass and feel the ground beneath you.
- Pray or read a single inspiring quote or scripture and reflect on how it applies to today.
- Try a one-minute guided breathing exercise, such as box breathing.

- Look out a window and find one detail you've never noticed before.
- Give yourself a hand massage or apply lotion slowly and mindfully.

Regrouping Ideas: Medium (15–60 Minutes)

These pauses offer deeper recovery without requiring a full day away from responsibilities.

- Take a walk in nature—leave your headphones behind and notice the sights, sounds, and textures around you.
- Do a brain-friendly workout that elevates your heart rate without depleting you, like yoga, swimming, or cycling.
- Spend time on a hobby that absorbs you in a healthy way—painting, gardening, playing music, or cooking a new recipe.
- Read a chapter from a book purely for enjoyment.
- Declutter one small space that you use daily—your desk, a drawer, your car console.
- Visit a quiet café or library and write freely in a journal without editing yourself.
- Schedule a call with a friend who helps you feel more like yourself.
- Try a guided meditation or visualization session to reset your focus.
- Take an unhurried shower or bath.
- Visit a local farmers' market and buy something fresh to enjoy.

- Spend time with an animal—your own pet, or visit a shelter or farm.
- Listen to an inspiring podcast or audiobook in a comfortable, quiet spot.
- Do a gentle yoga or stretching sequence designed for relaxation.
- Put together a small photo album or digital slideshow of happy memories.

Large Regrouping Ideas: (Retreats, Sabbaticals, Deep Resets)

Extended resets allow your mind, body, and spirit to slow down, restore, and refocus.

- Book a personal retreat—where you can unplug and be in a restorative environment.
- Take a digital sabbatical for a weekend or longer to allow your nervous system to settle down.
- Enroll in a workshop or program that fuels creativity, leadership, or personal growth.
- Spend a week in nature—camping, hiking, or staying in a quiet, scenic location—without a packed agenda.
- Go on a spiritual retreat to deepen your sense of meaning and reconnect with your values.
- Use vacation time for true rest rather than errands— read, nap, and explore slowly.
- Join a service trip or volunteer project that aligns with your values, offering both perspective and renewal.

- Plan an extended family trip focused on shared experiences rather than sightseeing checklists.
- Arrange a sabbatical from work or leadership roles to reassess priorities.
- Spend a season pursuing a creative project you've always wanted to start—writing, painting, music, etc.
- Join a mastermind or peer-support group for intentional time with like-minded people.

Every regroup, no matter how small, is a choice to protect what matters most—your energy, your clarity, your capacity to show up. Don't wait until you feel burned out or depleted to use these ideas. Begin today, in the middle of your busy, beautiful, imperfect life.

When you give yourself permission to pause, you're not stepping away from your purpose—you're strengthening it. These moments of reset aren't a distraction from your calling; they make it sustainable.

As you move forward, keep listening to the signals your mind and body send you. Let this list be a reminder that regrouping is not a luxury or a last resort—it's a way of living that keeps you aligned, resilient, and ready for what's next.

Appendix B:
REGROUP Framework

Step	Description	Tips
R – Resilience Starts Within	*Strength is found In memories, not merely moments.* You've faced hard things before. That strength is still in you - whether you feel it or not. Build from there.	◆ Reflect on a past challenge you overcame. ◆ Write down what helped you get through it. ◆ Remind yourself: strength doesn't disappear.
E – Energy is Fuel	*Energy is precious and limited; we must optimize it.* Recognize your energy drains, refuel with rest and enjoy what genuinely restores you.	◆ Track what activities energize vs. drain you. ◆ Build in short, restorative breaks. ◆ Say "no" without guilt.
G – Guard Your Margin	*Healthy people have healthy boundaries.* Margin doesn't just happen - you have to make it, then fiercely protect it. It's the boundaries that keep you steady, clear, and able to show up fully.	◆ Block breathing room in your calendar. ◆ Protect your "me" time. ◆ Treat boundaries as essential, not optional.
R – Regulate Your Nervous System	*Staying present creates productive peace.* Use breath, movement, and grounding tools to calm your nervous system and think more clearly.	◆ Practice box breathing during stress. ◆ Move your body every hour. ◆ Keep sensory tools, calming scents or textures, nearby.
O – Operate from Alignment	*Your actions tell the world what you value.* Say "yes" to what reflects your values. Say "no" to what pulls you away from who you are.	◆ Identify your top 3 values. ◆ Pause before committing and ask, 'Is this aligned?' ◆ Revisit your 'why' weekly.
U – Update Your Thinking	*Renew Your Mind - Not every thought deserves a seat at the table.* Notice old, unhelpful Automatic Negative thoughts (ANTs). Replace them with thoughts that support growth and joy.	◆ Catch and reframe negative thoughts. ◆ Use affirmations grounded in truth. ◆ Ask, 'Is this thought true?'
P – Prioritize Brain Health	*Taking time for you IS caring for others.* Your brain is the command center behind it all - your decisions, thoughts, emotions, relationships, and capacity to regroup. Care for it daily.	◆ Drink quality water daily. ◆ Fuel your brain with nutrient-rich foods. ◆ Stay mentally active with learning or creativity.

Appendix C: Additional Resources

Recommended Reading

- *Change Your Brain Change Your Life* by Daniel G. Amen, MD
- *Boundaries for Leaders* by Dr. Henry Cloud
- *5 Types of Wealth* by Sahil Boome
- *Micro-Resilience* by Bonnie St. John and Allen P. Haines
- *The Upside of Stress* by Kelly McGonigal, Ph.D.
- *The Body Keeps the Score* by Bessel van der Kolk, M.D.
- *Tiny Habits* by BJ Fogg, Ph.D.
- *Think Again* by Adam Grant, Ph.D.
- *Permission to Be Bold* by Barbara Gustavson.

Endnotes

[1] *American Psychological Association.* "Compounding pressure: The mental health crisis and the workplace. Work and Well-Being Survey." Accessed September 24, 2025. https://www.apa.org/pubs/reports/work-well-being/compounding-pressure-2021.

[2] *Family Caregiver Alliance.* "Caregiver Health." Accessed September 22, 2025. https://www.caregiver.org/resource/caregiver-health/

[3] Shapiro J. *Frontiers in Psychology.* "Burning bright or burning out: a qualitative investigation of leader vitality." October 1, 2023. https://doi.org/10.3389/fpsyg.2023.1244089

[4] McGonigal, K. *The Upside of Stress.* (New York, NY: Avery) 2016.

[5] Gong, W., & Geertshuis, S. A. *Frontiers in Psychology.* "Distress and Eustress: An Analysis of the Stress Experiences of Offshore International Students." May 4, 2023. https://doi.org/10.3389/fpsyg.2023.1144767.

[6] Ledoux, K. *Journal of Advanced Nursing.* "Understanding compassion fatigue: understanding compassion." 2015. https://doi.org/10.1111/jan.12686.

[7] van der Kolk, B. A. *The Body Keeps the Score.* (New York, NY: Viking) 2014.

[8] Rohn, J., & Willingham, R. *The Seasons of Life.* (Dallas, TX: Jim Rohn International) 1981.

[9] Bratman, Gregory N.; Hamilton, J. Paul; Hahn, Kevin S. *PNAS* "Nature Experience Reduces Rumination and Subgenual Prefrontal Cortex Activation." June 29, 2015. https://www.pnas.org/doi/10.1073/pnas.1510459112

[10] I. Oswald, "Review of Sleep and Wakefulness, by Nathaniel Kleitman," *Electroencephalography and Clinical Neurophysiology* 18, no. 3 (1965): 320, https://doi.org/10.1016/0013-4694(65)90104-5.

[11] S. J. Kingsbury, "Review of The Psychobiology of Mind-Body Healing: New Concepts of Therapeutic Hypnosis, rev. ed., edited by Ernest Lawrence Rossi," *General Hospital Psychiatry* 16, no. 6 (1994): 438–39, https://doi.org/10.1016/0163-8343(94)90122-8.

[12] Grant, A. *Think Again.* (New York, NY: Viking) 2021.

[13] Siegel, D. J. *The Developing Mind.* (New York, NY: Guilford Press) 1999.

[14] Petruccelli, K., Davis, J., & Berman, T. *Child Abuse and Neglect.* "Adverse childhood experiences and associated health outcomes: A systematic review and meta-analysis." 2019. https://doi.org/10.1016/j.chiabu.2019.104127

[15] Tedeschi, R. G., & Calhoun, L. G. *Journal of Traumatic Stress* "The posttraumatic growth inventory: Measuring the positive legacy of trauma." 1996. https://doi.org/10.1002/jts.2490090305

[16] Lamb, Susan. *National Library of Medicine.* "Neuroplasticity: a century-old idea championed by Adolf Meyer." December 9, 2019. https://pmc.ncbi.nlm.nih.gov/articles/PMC6901269/.

[17] St. John, B., & Haines, A. *Micro-resilience*. (New York, NY: Center Street) 2017.

[18] Arnsten, A. F. T. *Nature Reviews Neuroscience*. "Stress signalling pathways that impair prefrontal cortex structure and function." June 2009. https://doi.org/10.1038/nrn2648.

[19] Cloud, Henry. *Boundaries for Leaders: Results, Relationships, and Being Ridiculously in Charge*. (HarperBusiness: NY, NY) 2013.

[20] Lamontagne, A. D.; Keegel, T.; Louie, A. M.; Ostry, A.; & Landsbergis, P. A. *International Journal of Environmental Research and Public Health*. "A Systematic Review of the Job-stress Intervention Evaluation Literature, 1990–2005." July 19, 2013. https://doi.org/10.1179/oeh.2007.13.3.268.

[21] Derks, D., & Bakker, A. B. *Applied Psychology*. "Smartphone Use, Work-home Interference, and Burnout: A Diary Study on the Role of Recovery." October 31, 2012. https://doi.org/10.1111/j.1464-0597.2012.00530.x.

[22] McEwen, B. S., & Morrison, J. H. *Neuron*. "The Brain on Stress: Vulnerability and Plasticity of the Prefrontal Cortex Over the Life Course." July 10, 2013. https://doi.org/10.1016/j.neuron.2013.06.028.

[23] Schwartz, J. M., & Begley, S. *The Mind and the Brain: Neuroplasticity and the Power of Mental Force*. (New York, NY: Harper Perennial) 2002.

[24] Porges, S. W. *The Polyvagal Theory* (1st ed.). (New York, NY: W. W. Norton) 2011.

[25] *Khiron Clinic*. "Finding the Ventral Vagal State." Accessed September 18, 2025. https://khironclinics.com/blog/finding-the-ventral-vagal-state/.

[26] Tang, Y. Y.; Hölzel, B. K.; & Posner, M. I. *Nature Reveiws Science*. "The neuroscience of mindfulness meditation." March 18, 2015. https://doi.org/10.1038/nrn3916.

27   Thoma, M. V., Ryf, S.; Mohiyeddini, C.; Ehlert, U., & Nater, U. M. *Cognition and Emotion.* "Emotion regulation through listening to music in everyday situations." (2013) https://doi.org/10.1080/02699931.2012.750235

28   Hunter, M. R.; Gillespie, B. W.; & Chen, S. Y. *Frontiers in Psychology.* "Urban nature experiences reduce stress in the context of daily life based on salivary biomarkers." 2019. https://doi.org/10.3389/fpsyg.2019.00722.

29   Pennebaker, J. W.; & Smyth, J. M. Opening up by writing it down: How expressive writing improves health and eases emotional pain. (New York, NY: Guilford Press) 2019.

30   Jain, S., Shapirol; S. L., Swanick; S., Roesch, S. C., Mills; P. J., Bell, I.; & Schwartz, G. E. *Annals of Behavorial Medicine.* "A randomized controlled trial of mindfulness meditation versus relaxation training: Effects on distress, positive states of mind, rumination, and distraction." 2019. https://doi.org/10.1207/s15324796abm3301_2.

31   Coan, J. A.; Schaefer, H. S.; & Davidson R. J. *Psychological Science.* "Lending a hand: Social regulation of the neural response to threat." 2016. https://doi.org/10.1111/j.1467-9280.2006.01832.x.

32   David, S. Emotional agility: Get unstuck, embrace change, and thrive in work and life. (New York, NY: Avery) 2016.

33   Amen, D. G. *The End of Mental Illness.* (Carol Stream, IL: Tyndale Momentum) 2020.

34   Beck, A. T. *Cognitive Therapy and the Emotional Disorders.* (New York: International Universities Press) 1976.

35   Burns, D. D. *Feeling Good: The New Mood Therapy.* (New York, NY: William Morrow) 1980.

36   Beck, A. T. *Archives of General Psychiatry.* "The Current State of Cognitive Therapy: A 40-year Retrospective. 2005. https://doi.org/10.1001/archpsyc.62.9.953.

[37]   Amen, D. G. *Change Your Brain, Change Your Life.* (New York, NY: Three Rivers Press) 1999.

[38]   Fredrickson, Barbara L., "The Role of Positive Emotions in Positive Psychology: The Broaden-and-Build Theory of Positive Emotions," *American Psychologist* 56, no. 3 (2001): 218–26, https://doi.org/10.1037/0003-066X.56.3.218.

[39]   Byron, K., & Mitchell, S. *Loving What Is.* (Nevada City, CA: Harmony Books) 2002.

[40]   *Amen Clinics.* "12 Brain Health Principles." May 5, 2020. https://www.amenclinics.com/blog/the-12-underlying-principles-of-amen-clinics/.

[41]   Amen, D. G. *Change Your Brain, Change Your Life.* (New York, NY: Three Rivers Press) 2015.

[42]   Bryant Fred B., Veroff Joseph. *Savoring: A new model of positive experience.* (East Sussex, England: Psychology Press) 2006.

[43]   Abramson, Ashley. *American Psychological Association.* "Hope as the Antidote." January 1, 2024. https://www.apa.org/monitor/2024/01/trends-hope-greater-meaning-life.

Acknowledgments

Igniting Souls Writing Team–Thank you for your wisdom, encouragement, and guidance in helping me bring these words to life.

Launch Team–Thank you to those who were willing to read my book and offer honest feedback. Your support means more than you know.

To those who allowed me to share their story–Thank you for your vulnerability and for the impact you're making in the world.

Mom, Dad, and Angie–Though I miss you every day, the strength, pain, and resilience I carry were forged in the love and life we shared. Thank you for shaping me into who I am today.

Paul, Taylor, Michael, and Wani–You hold my heart. Your love and unwavering support have been my anchor and my joy. Being a wife and mom is my greatest accomplishment.

My care team–To my therapist, coaches, and friends, thank you for holding space for me, for your honesty, and for your faith in me. You've been part of my healing and growth in more ways than I can name.

Gail - Thank you for being my mom's best friend and for walking with me through my parents' journeys. I could not have done it without your unwavering support.

Dr. Daniel Amen–Thank you for your friendship and for changing the way the world views mental health. You helped shift the trajectory of my life.

My Amen University team and colleagues–Thank you for being partners in purpose. Your passion, collaboration, and shared commitment to brain health has made this work deeply meaningful.

The clinicians, coaches, students, and graduates I work with–Your courage, stories, and relentless hope inspire me every day. You are the heartbeat of this work.

My clients–Thank you for trusting me with your stories, your hopes, and your healing journeys. Your courage to show up, do the work, and choose growth has deeply impacted me. You've taught me as much as I've guided you, and I carry your resilience with me in everything I create.

Friends and mentors who believed in me when I questioned myself–Your words have carried me through seasons I couldn't have navigated alone.

Readers and supporters–Thank you for walking this journey with me. Your willingness to grow and live your life with purpose is why this book exists.

About the Author

Barbara Gustavson is a brain health educator, speaker, and leadership facilitator with a Master's in Psychology. Known for her down-to-earth approach and calming presence, she equips community leaders, caregivers, and health professionals with practical, science-backed tools to regroup, rewire, and lead with clarity.

Her work blends neuroscience, psychology, and human connection to help others prevent burnout, build resilience, and lead sustainably. She oversees Dr. Daniel Amen's brain health certification programs and is the author of Permission to Be Bold and co-author of Breaking Average.

Barbara Gustavson has worked with coaches, clinicians, and educators around the world to integrate brain-based strategies into their work. She's also partnered with organizations to support corporate wellness, stress management, and culture change from the inside out.

Known for her relatable presence and deep understanding of hidden stressors, her work offers a practical path forward rooted in both science and compassion. Barbara brings clarity and alignment to her workshops, keynotes, and consulting, and she meets people where they are—especially those who have a big calling and carry heavy loads.

With a B.S. in Management and an M.S. in Psychology, Barbara equips her audiences with science-backed tools to reset their energy, reframe stress, and lead with their authentic selves.

Connect with Barbara at DiscoverNextStep.com.

INSPIRING LEADERS TO REGROUP, REFOCUS, AND REBUILD

From community leaders and caregivers to health and wellness professionals—audiences connect with Barbara's warm, strength-based approach to resilience, brain health, and sustainable leadership.

Whether you're navigating stress, transition, or simply trying to lead with a full plate, Barbara offers practical tools to reset your mind and restore energy from the inside out.

She helps audiences:

- Lead with clarity—even when life feels messy
- Recover energy without abandoning their purpose
- Reframe stress as a signal— not a setback

Blending neuroscience, psychology, and lived insight, Barbara delivers a message that feels personal and doable. Attendees leave with clarity, encouragement, and actionable next steps.

SCAN TO LEARN MORE OR BOOK BARBARA FOR YOUR NEXT EVENT:

DiscoverNextStep.com/Speaking